PAWPRINTS *of* KATRINA

PETS SAVED AND LESSONS LEARNED

CATHY SCOTT

PHOTOGRAPHY BY CLAY MYERS

WILEY
Wiley Publishing, Inc.

Library of Congress Cataloging-in-Publication Data:

Scott, Cathy.
  Pawprints of Katrina : pets saved and lessons learned / Cathy Scott ; photography by Clay Myers.
    p. cm.
  ISBN 978-0-470-22851-7
1. Animal rescue—Louisiana—New Orleans. 2. Pets—Louisiana—New Orleans. 3. Hurricane Katrina, 2005. I. Title.
  HV4765.L8S26 2008
  636.08'32–dc22
                              2008001402

Printed in the United States of America

10 9 8 7 6 5 4 3 2

Book design by Erin Zeltner

Cover design by Wendy Mount

Book production by Wiley Publishing, Inc. Composition Services

To the people and pets of the Gulf Coast—
those we helped and those we couldn't.
Because of them, animals will never again be
forgotten in a disaster.

And to my father, the late James M. Scott, a
hillbilly kid at heart from the Ozarks of
Missouri, who passed on his love of all living
creatures to his five children.

Contents

Foreword

When the devastating tragedy of Hurricane Katrina struck New Orleans in August 2005, the whole world watched as countless heartbreaking, indelible images and stories were broadcast on our television and computer screens. Among them were the unforgettable faces of the thousands of animals left stranded by the terrible storm and the all-too-fragile levees.

We did what we could to help, but there were people and organizations who performed real miracles. Among these was the Utah-based Best Friends Animal Society, whose rescue work is chronicled in this beautiful book by Cathy Scott. She was one of the volunteers who rushed to the scene to help rescue seven thousand terrified, abandoned animals and to follow through with medical and emotional support. Cathy stayed in New Orleans for nearly four months, leaving an important university teaching job in Las Vegas to continue working with and writing about the animals. This book is partly her story, but ultimately it is the animals' story. It is also about one group of people who worked exhaustively to reconnect some six hundred pets with their original owners and to organize foster homes and permanent adoptions for more than six thousand others.

As a lifelong animal lover and activist, I am moved to tears by these stories and by the photographs of Clay Myers. *Pawprints of Katrina* is an unforgettable account of the courage and boundless energy of people who realize that we human beings have an absolute obligation to help the other creatures of this planet. In seeing these images and reading the accounts in this book, we are reminded of the very best behavior of which the human heart is capable.

I love this book.

Ali MacGraw

Preface

In late August 2005, Hurricane Katrina slammed into the Gulf Coast region, flattening towns and cities and turning New Orleans into an uninhabitable, toxic swamp. In the days immediately following, tens of thousands of pets were left stranded without food or water, their owners expecting to return to them in two or three days.

One week later, I volunteered to go to the region, and Best Friends Animal Society agreed, sending me down as an embedded reporter to write for its Web site and magazine. By early September, I was on the ground documenting the rescue effort.

As word spread, with footage of marooned animals airing each day around the world, those wanting to help flocked to the Gulf, in the same way that I was drawn to the area. Afterward, when I returned home, I was haunted by the stories of the pets and the particulars of their lives. As both a journalist and an animal lover, one who shares a home with rescued and fostered dogs, those stories struck a personal note. I felt lucky to have gone down to the region with a professional rescue group to witness the first massive animal roundup. And I wanted to put on paper what I'd seen.

Best Friends Animal Society was the first into the area—the first to arrive in boats to rescue animals from the floodwaters—and the last to leave. It was nearly nine months before the largest no-kill sanctuary in the United States, based on thirty-three thousand acres in Kanab, Utah, would pull out of the region, waiting until the last dogs and cats were either reunited with their people or placed in new homes. All told, Best Friends' teams rescued roughly seven thousand pets. Between the various rescue groups, it is estimated that some fifteen thousand—possibly more—domestic animals were saved from the ruins.

The pets rescued by Best Friends were taken to a center erected on the grounds of the St. Francis Animal Sanctuary in Tylertown, Mississippi, ninety miles north of New Orleans. During the storm, the sanctuary lost its electricity because of the winds. A day after the storm, Best Friends arrived in the region. In less than a week, they had assembled a crew that brought in generators, fixed fencing, and repaired runs. They set up their own animal relief center—called Camp Tylertown—on the St. Francis property and began going into New Orleans each day to pluck animals from the water, rubble, and ensuing muck. At the end of each day the animals were taken to Camp Tylertown, where they were treated and cared for.

The rescue events that unfolded in the wreckage of Katrina were marked by the refugee pets' tremendous will to live. Whatever the circumstances—in the water, on the streets, inside homes or locked schools—many animals ended up the winners, despite their needs being ignored because of an official order forbidding residents from evacuating with their companion pets.

A percentage of animals not only survived, but, in large part because of the love and care afforded to them by their two-legged friends, also moved on to live happy, healthy lives. New federal legislation means they will never again have to be abandoned during a crisis. Moreover, rescue groups will be behind the scenes at the next disaster, reminding officials of their commitment to the animals.

Although my enthusiasm for Best Friends Animal Society is evident throughout these pages, it does not discount the extraordinary efforts made by many other groups and individuals who did their part in making a difference in so many pets' lives. And if I anthropomorphize the pet victims, that's because it's difficult to scientifically describe love.

The pets left behind have become symbols of the courageous spirit of those who endured the events that unfolded on the Gulf Coast. Events themselves can't be courageous; people or animals can be. These are their stories, from my frontline vantage point and from the lens of photographer Clay Myers.

1

The Water

O N THE WATER'S EDGE, from a ramp leading from Interstate 10, I looked out on a vast span of still but deadly black water surrounding a New Orleans neighborhood. It was like a scene out of *Waterworld*, a postapocalyptic science fiction film. The off-ramp had been transformed into a boat launch. The silence was otherworldly.

Driving to the area that morning meant passing by one of the city's oldest cemeteries not far from the French Quarter, with its aboveground nineteenth-century marble, brick-and-mortar, and stone tombs topped with Christian symbols of angels and crosses. The scene was eerie as the flooded tombs appeared to float in the watery sludge.

It was September 11, 2005. Parked on the ramp and sitting on the tailgate of his truck was Captain Scott Shields of the New York City Fire Department, famous for the courageous efforts of his search-and-rescue dog, Bear, at the World Trade Center. Captain Scott was with special boat teams deployed to the Gulf Coast region on behalf of the Bear Search and Rescue Foundation in memory of his dog, who, like many other working canines, passed away from health complications developed after searching Ground Zero following the September 11, 2001, terrorist attacks.

Before we set out on a boat to look for stranded pets, the captain looked around at the Best Friends Animal Society team. Then he asked us to take a moment to remember those lost on 9/11. There, standing amidst the rubble of Hurricane Katrina with the black water just a few feet from us, we bowed our heads, and not a sound was heard. No cars. No lawnmowers. No birds. No planes. No trains. No voices. Not even the couple of dogs

rescued and then tied with leashes to the off-ramp railing, awaiting transport, uttered a sound. It was as if, at that brief but
somber point in time, they, too, acknowledged the loss of life.
It was a poignant moment, observing those lost in the largest
terrorist attack on American soil while we were in the thick of
rescuing animals in the wake of the biggest natural disaster in
U.S. history. The Crescent City was devoid of life, except for those
of us out rescuing that day and, of course, the animals left
behind.

Leaving in boats were Jeff Popowich, Ethan Gurney, and Mike
Bzdewka, all with the Best Friends organization, and volunteers
Ken Ray and Tracey Simmons. Volunteer veterinarian Debbie
Rykoff stayed on the ramp to treat the pets brought in from the
water.

I stepped into a small, aluminum jon boat—stable and flat-
bottomed—with Mike and Tracey, and we motored away from the
freeway toward the nearby houses, maneuvering around felled
trees, fallen street signs, water-logged cars, and whatever else was
in the water. We boated out to a five-block area and stopped at
Myrtle Street.

It was my first run of the day and Mike and Tracey's second.
Mike cut the engine, and we sat in the boat with silence all
around us. "Watch this," Tracey said as she started barking.
"Woof, woof, woof." The street lit up with the sounds of animals.
We heard a cat meow from three blocks away. On Myrtle, a
dog barked, and then we heard another cat. At the intersection, Mike stepped out of the boat to pull us past large debris
and tree trunks, and then he jumped back in and continued
motoring.

It was an older neighborhood of wooden row houses, and the
water was just above the porches. We boated to the first house on
the corner, where we'd heard a cat meow from inside. Mike
stepped onto the porch, opened a window, and grabbed the cat.
He put the cat in a pillowcase, because we didn't have a carrier,
and handed it to me as he got back in the boat. I set the cat next

to me on the bench seat so he wouldn't get wet from the polluted water on the floor of the boat.

Midway down the street, a dog barked from a backyard. We moved toward the narrow driveway on the side of the house and saw a gray Poodle mix on a car roof next to piled-high debris that used to be a garage. Mike got out and waded to the house next door while I stayed in the boat with the cat. I held onto a porch railing with one hand and petted the cat through the pillowcase with the other. Tracey stepped out and, wearing rubber hip waders, began making her way down the driveway. Halfway, she abruptly stopped and let out a moan.

"Are you okay?" I called out.

"No," she hollered back. "Something's in the water." She was quiet for a moment, and then she said, "I think it's a body."

"If it was a body, it would be floating," I told her.

"It's bubbling. It just moved," she said, lifting her arms above her head.

I knew she was spooking herself even more, so I tried to change her focus. "Look around you, Tracey," I said. "See the tree branches sticking out of the water? It's just a tree trunk."

"Are you sure?" she asked.

"Positive," I told her, not sure of anything at that point. "Just focus on the dog. Keep looking at the dog and step over the tree."

She slowly started moving again. It seemed like it took an eternity for her to reach the car. When she did, the dog jumped over the rubble behind him and into the murky water. Finally, she cornered him, plucked him from the muck, and carefully waded up the driveway and back to the boat. Tracey said she thought it might have been an alligator, because there were reports of sightings, but we doubted a gator could survive in that murky muck.

The still-wet dog, who turned out to be a Cockapoo we later named Goofy, sat on my lap and didn't move, even with the cat next to him. We got a second cat from next door, and then went to a few more houses on the street. Tracey followed Mike into one house, but she didn't have a good feeling and turned around. When Mike emerged, he told us that five dogs had been tied in the yard, and it looked like they had all drowned when the water rose higher than their leashes could reach.

In silence, we motored away from Myrtle to Elder Street, to where a cat was walking on a rooftop. We called to him, but he walked even higher to the roof's peak. The fence was down, and there was no way for us to climb up. He was out of reach, so we headed back to the boat ramp, hoping another team with more gear could get him.

That scene played out every day on rescue duty. So did the sight of animals who hadn't made it. On the front of one house in Lakeview, spray-painted in black were the words "4 dead dogs on log chains in back yard." The teams learned to celebrate the successes and not dwell on the animals we could no longer help. It was the same with the people who had died and whose bodies were floating in the water. There wasn't anything left for us to do for them.

Because floodwater was steadily receding from neighborhoods throughout the city, rescue teams geared up for door-to-door searches on land where the waterline was dropping and for boat searches in areas where the water was still waist deep.

I had arrived two days earlier, on September 9, 2005, when my plane landed in Jackson, Mississippi. By noon the next day, I was at Camp Tylertown, where Best Friends had set up an animal triage center. I immediately went to work on the fifty-acre grounds of the St. Francis Animal Sanctuary, a place that was alive with activity.

Assignments often lead journalists in their careers. Stories of the military have taken me to Somalia, Saudi Arabia, and Panama. In the case of Katrina, instead of human strife, the plight of helpless animals took me to the hurricane-ravaged Gulf region. When the opportunity arose to travel to New Orleans, Biloxi, Waveland, and Gulfport to cover the largest animal rescue effort in history, I jumped at the chance. Within a day and a half, I was there, recording the events and stories of the displaced pets of Katrina.

I stayed from September to November 2005, returned a month later, and then returned again in January 2006. I went back for one last trip in May 2006 to cover Best Friends' pullout from the region.

I'll never forget being told by Kristi Littrell, an adoption coordinator at Best Friends Animal Society's Utah headquarters, where 1,800 animals live on any given day: "Watch over the little ones for me." And I did, as best I could, almost from the start.

That first afternoon I went inside Kitty City, a cabinlike building that was used as a cattery. The rooms, except for two in the back, had been emptied to make space for a dual-purpose office, triage overflow area, and storage for medical supplies. On a screened-in patio at the back of the building, where the temperature was about 110 degrees, some crates housed a handful of small dogs in triage, because there was nowhere else to put them.

A volunteer and I walked through in search of a red Pomeranian whose owner was desperately looking for her. Inside one of the crates, we found the dog, whose name was Brooklyn. She was in good shape. I was about to leave the patio to notify the command center that I'd located Brooklyn when I noticed another small dog, this one a thin, balding, friendly four-pound Chihuahua puppy inside a nearby kennel. She wagged her tail and was so happy to see me, despite her pink skin, itchy from fleabites, and the mucus on her nose and eyes. She was panting, but she also sneezed and appeared to have kennel cough. I retrieved her from the crate and walked her over to the small building next door that was dubbed the M*A*S*H Unit—a makeshift emergency hospital—and asked a veterinary technician if I could keep her with me.

I later learned from Pam Perez, who cofounded the St. Francis Sanctuary with her daughter, that they had picked up the puppy, along with five other Chihuahuas and four Basset-and-Beagle-mix dogs, from a yard on the outskirts of Franklinton, Louisiana, about twenty miles south of Tylertown. It was a run-down wooden home on a corner lot where the residents had been breeding dogs in their backyard . . . literally. According to neighbors, they'd moved three weeks before the storm, taking some of the animals with them but leaving twenty-one alone in the yard. The Chihuahua puppy and the others toughed out the hurricane by themselves on that lot. Pam rescued ten, and another rescue group in the area took the remaining eleven.

A volunteer and I gave the puppy a bath in antiseptic shampoo and put aloe on her flea-bitten skin, and I took her under my wing. Even so, that first night, she scratched her skin for hours, and neither of us slept. Because the power was still off at the St. Francis Sanctuary, the dog and I spent those first two nights in a sleeping bag on the porch of the main building, which was also cabinlike. The next day, I gave the puppy an oatmeal bath to help relieve the itching. It worked, and her skin began to heal. Dr. Pema Mallu, a holistic veterinarian and Buddhist nun from Arizona, gave the pup a probiotic to relieve her kennel cough symptoms and boost her immune system.

The little dog rested on my lap as I sat on the porch, writing articles that chronicled both the rescue efforts and life at Camp Tylertown. I named the little Chihuahua Lois Lane, because I looked at her as my cub reporter. Once the power—and the lights—were back on, Lois Lane and I moved into the building and slept on the floor of the laundry area.

Each morning during that first week, Lois Lane got up from under the covers of our bed on the floor and picked a spot on a lower shelf where towels and sheets were stacked against a wall, making herself a cozy bed as she patiently waited for me to get ready for the day. She became quite a hit with the volunteers. I couldn't put her down on the grass to walk her in front of the buildings because of the bacteria and diseases the animals were bringing in from the streets, so I carried her everywhere with me, except when I'd put her down on the lawn across from the gravel road that ran through the sanctuary. Lois Lane stayed with me during my first deployment—a two-month stint—in Tylertown and later went home with me as a foster dog. She was eventually adopted out to Best Friends employees Pat and Larry Donoho, who had her treated for heartworm after we learned that Lois had tested positive for the disease.

Two days after I'd gone into the field for the first time, a team picked up a stray Shih Tzu mom during a sweep of a neighborhood. With her was a male terrier mix. Elissa Jones, a Best Friends staff member, discovered the mother and took her to Dr. Debbie Rykoff, who accompanied the team that day in the van. Dr. Deb knew instantly that the female dog was still nursing. "She has puppies somewhere," she told Elissa.

So Elissa walked the mama dog on a leash to where she had first spotted her. Sure enough, the mother led Elissa straight to her two newborn pups on the second floor of a house, out of sight from the street. The puppies looked to be about ten days old and in good condition. That evening, Elissa and the team took the mother and pups to Camp Tylertown.

Three days later, on September 16, another team deployed by Best Friends, accompanied this time by a couple of professional responders along with a Best Friends rapid response team, went into St. Bernard Parish, located south of New Orleans, where most of the area was flooded with between four and fourteen feet of standing water.

The Best Friends team was the first animal rescue group allowed into the area after the storm. Prior to that time, officials wouldn't let anyone besides law enforcement into St. Bernard Parish, despite the thousands of pets still alive in and around homes. That first day, the rescue team pulled sixty pets from the area, twenty-nine of which were cats. Despite what they'd been through, the animals were in relatively good shape, surprising everyone.

Best Friends' first water extraction team was in the water a little more than a week after the storm and continued into the third week when it gradually went from a water operation to a ground operation. In some spots in those early days, there were islands of dry ground. In other areas, a combination of water and thick oil coated the streets.

Paul Berry, then chief operating officer for Best Friends, had arrived in New Orleans the morning the first levee broke. When Paul, who grew up in New Orleans, saw the extensive damage and learned that residents hadn't been allowed to take their pets when they evacuated, he quickly dispatched a Best Friends rapid response team to help the animals. That phone call prompted a domino effect that resulted in the creation of Camp Tylertown, the base site on the grounds of the St. Francis Animal Sanctuary where volunteers soon arrived in droves wanting nothing more than to help. At the Best Friends headquarters in southern Utah, a command center, run by Anne Mejia, was simultaneously put in place and staffed.

As for the St. Francis Sanctuary, the storm touched down in Tylertown at daybreak on Monday, September 1. "The sun was coming up and it was bearing down on us," sanctuary cofounder Heidi Krupp said. They found out how bad it was in New Orleans by listening to their car radios. They had no electricity and, because the pumps needed power to run, they were without water. "My mom drove out to Tylertown and McComb looking for bottled water to give the animals," Heidi said. They had roughly six hundred animals already living at the sanctuary when the storm hit. Even so, Heidi said, "We made an agreement right away with Paul that animals he rescued would come here."

That's what happened almost immediately. On Friday, September 2, Jefferson Parish Animal Control officers delivered more than a hundred evacuated dogs and cats that were being temporarily housed in crates at the county fairgrounds in Franklinton, Louisiana. Once they were moved to base camp, some dogs were placed in available runs at the sanctuary. Others were kept in their kennels, waiting for fencing to arrive with the

Best Friends team members, who were on their way. The cats were placed inside at the sanctuary's Kitty City.

A day and a half later, on Sunday morning, the Best Friends team—Ethan Gurney, a former Marine; Troy Snow, a photographer; and Russ Mead, the general counsel and crisis manager—drove a trailer, a van, and a truck, respectively, onto the sanctuary grounds. The vehicles were loaded with temporary fencing, food (for people and animals), generators, satellite phones, and fuel. The first thing the team did was erect the fencing so the dogs delivered from Jefferson Parish could be moved from crates to runs.

Also that day, the first volunteers arrived at the St. Francis shelter. "At eleven thirty at night, these people pulled into our lots with a trailer behind them," Heidi said. "They had two trucks, and they were full of dog food."

The following Tuesday, when Alabama volunteer Ken Ray arrived with his boat, the team hit the water, putting the boat in from on- and off-ramps along Interstate 10. That began the steady three-month flow of rescued animals arriving each day at base camp from New Orleans, where volunteers were streaming in.

In the field, National Guard and Coast Guard members were doing what they could, too. One dog—a seven-week-old black Lab puppy—was plucked from the dark water by the Coast Guard. A rescue team that included Dr. Debbie Rykoff was in the field that day and met up with the Coast Guard officers at an off-ramp by I-10 not far from the 610 Freeway. The only sign of life for miles, the puppy clung to a clump of weeds, a tiny black speck in the toxic soup. The soldiers fed her scraps of food left over from their rations of Meals Ready to Eat (MREs). "The weeds were the only thing that saved her from drowning," said Dr. Deb, who eventually took the puppy she named Surreal back home with her to Chicago.

While Camp Tylertown was still being set up, Best Friends, through an agreement with the Jefferson Parish shelter's temporary site in Tarlington, pulled animals from the parish's shelter and took them to base camp. As they arrived, workers from both

Best Friends and St. Francis, along with a few volunteers, quickly erected temporary fencing. While at the Jefferson Parish shelter a week after the storm, Paul witnessed a female American Pit Bull Terrier nursing two different litters of puppies. The scene, he later said, captured the spirit of what was going on throughout the Gulf Coast region: neighbor helping neighbor.

After Katrina hit, 80 percent of New Orleans and many of its neighboring parishes were left underwater. The majority of rescues were carried out from small boats, picking up dogs and cats from rooftops, off floating debris—sometimes having to use wire cutters to extricate the pets—and from second-floor windows and attic openings. Many residents were fishermen who used their working boats to retrieve neighbors and their pets stranded in homes and on rooftops.

Ripper and Domino, Pit Bull mixes, were two such pets, stranded on a car roof in a driveway behind a mangled chain-link fence near the city. As the Best Friends boat turned the corner onto the dogs' street, Ripper wasn't taking any chances. He dove into the dark water and met his rescuers. What Ripper did not realize was that the boat, with rescuers Jeff Popowich, Ethan Gurney, and Troy Snow on board, was already headed their way.

Still, Ripper dove into the murky floodwater with his purpose clear; he wasn't letting the boat leave without him. His look said it all: *Not here, not today.* A few minutes later, Ripper was pulled from the water and lifted to safety, and then the team continued toward the car to retrieve Domino.

Once at Camp Tylertown, Ripper's caregivers knew him at Pooch Alley, a section of base camp where Pit Bulls were housed, as the vocal dog who talked to them in a high-pitched bark. Some called him Screecher. He was also the dog who ripped apart a kiddy pool each time it was put in his run and filled with water—thus the name Ripper.

"He was still very puppyish in his behavior," said Sherry Woodard, an animal expert who oversaw animal care at base camp. "He would climb all over people and be very sweet. But he would eat any kind of plastic bowl and put teeth marks in metal bowls."

What he needed, Sherry said, was direction. "I knew that if he didn't get into the right hands, he would be in trouble." So Sherry sent him home with Leah Purcell, who runs Spindletop Pit Bull Refuge in Houston. Leah knew a trainer who could foster and work with Ripper.

Ripper, who was about ten months old when he was rescued, "now knows how to control himself," Sherry said. "He's a trained tracking dog." He also went through extensive obedience training. Because of the advanced training, coupled with his young age, Sherry said he'd be a good candidate for police or search-and-rescue work.

Ripper will continue to live on several acres with his foster mom, no matter how long it takes to place him. "I visit him on a regular basis," Leah said. "He gets to run a lot during the day, playing with his indestructible ball."

Domino, the black-and-white Pit Bull who had been stranded with Ripper on the roof of the car, went to Spindletop as well, and was adopted out a couple of months later to a north Texas family with two teenagers and a male dog named Jagger.

Two other Pit Bulls—Piglet, a white, pink-nosed female, and an unnamed male with a brown-marble-colored coat—were also together, but on a sinking boat still attached to a trailer in a driveway when they were rescued. Doctor Deb, with the crew that day, waited in her rented SUV on the ramp for the dogs and cats to be boated to her so she could treat them. Piglet was dehydrated and had superficial cuts on her face and head, so Deb immediately hooked her up to IV fluids. Collapsed on a blanket in the SUV, Piglet lay there quietly as Dr. Deb worked on her.

Once at Camp Tylertown, workers took good care of Piglet. Volunteer Momi Ford, who worked Pooch Alley with a group of five women, remembers naming her. "Piglet was in the first pen right next to our supply tent, which we dubbed the Monkey Lounge," Momi said. "I was going down the rows coming up with names for the dogs when another volunteer, Jan Mintun, was pulling a hose down in the opposite direction. Piglet was so excited to have our attention, she would smile and snort and wiggle when we came near. As Jan pulled the hose down the row, she looked back and said something to her like, 'You're just a little Miss Piggy, aren't you?' I looked at her, and the image of Piglet from *Winnie the Pooh* came to mind immediately." After that, everyone called the dog Piglet.

Each day during her ten-day stint at camp, Momi applied sunscreen to Piglet's skin to protect her from the harsh sun. "I went into her pen first thing every morning and again during the day to put suntan lotion all over her," Momi said. "She loved it. I'd go up to her pen with the bottle of lotion and ask her if she wanted some sunscreen rubbed on her. She would give me that great, huge smile of hers and just wiggle and snort. It was impossible to keep her clean, though, as she would just wriggle around in the dirt in ecstasy from all the attention."

Piglet, who had heartworm disease, was fostered by volunteer veterinarian Karen Michalsi, who drove the dog from base camp to Serenity Animal Hospital in Sterling Heights, Michigan. After heartworm treatments, Piglet eventually passed an intermediate obedience course, and, just before the first anniversary of Katrina, she was adopted to Angenette Graham in Detroit, where she is the only dog in the house.

Another white Pit Bull was found on September 9 in a bright-blue boat near a freeway off-ramp. A Best Friends rescue team leaving the city for the day ran across a National Guard unit who told them a dog was inside a boat off Interstate 10. Someone had spray painted the words "Dog in Boat" in red letters on the side of the small vessel. When the rescue team (which included Paul Berry, Kit Boggio, and Troy Snow) spotted the boat just off the freeway, they headed toward it. A bag of dry dog food had been left in the boat, but diesel fuel had spilled into the hull and saturated it. The dog, too, was covered in fuel. She was sunburned and blistered. Back at base camp, she was cleaned up and named Diesel, and spent her first couple of evenings sitting on the porch with Kit. She was eventually fostered out to an individual who volunteered at Camp Tylertown.

A picture of Diesel being rescued ran on the cover of a book by photographer Troy Snow and released by Best Friends titled *Not Left Behind*. After Coast Guard Lieutenant Brandon Guldseth saw the book, he tried to get in touch with someone who could give him more information about Diesel. Seeing a story I'd written about Diesel that was posted on the Internet, on March 1, 2007, the officer sent me an e-mail.

Hello,

My name is Brandon Guldseth, a Lieutenant Junior Grade Officer in the United States Coast Guard. I believe we were the first ones to find "Diesel" in the damaged blue boat alongside the highway in New Orleans. The first time that I saw her, she kind of startled me. We were using that on-ramp as a deployment point to effect Search and Rescue operations of people. I leaned against the boat and glanced into it. To my surprise, there was a dog in there and I took a step back. I was saddened by the condition of her. She had lesions and bumps all over her legs and was severely dehydrated. I wanted to take her right there and then, but our mission was a different one at the time and I knew that I could not take her. We tried to give her some bottled water, but she would not drink any. It was my crewman who spray-painted "DOG IN BOAT" on the side of the boat with a spray can that we found lying next to it.

I am a dog lover and I grew up with a Newfoundland and a German Shepherd. I was tortured mentally by the condition of the dogs in New Orleans and the way their owners would just abandon them, just as they did Diesel. I never knew what happened to her and I was fearful that she had died a horrible death. Just yesterday I was in a local bookstore in Belleville, Illinois, near St. Louis, Missouri, which is where I am stationed in the Coast Guard. Searching through the dog section, I noticed the book *Not Left Behind*.

Flipping through the pages in the book reminded me of the locations that still haunt me to this day. When I got to the middle of the book, I saw the expanded picture of "Dog In Boat." I turned to the next page and saw "Diesel" being rescued. I wanted to cry right there in the middle of the store because I felt relieved and saddened all at the same time. Here in the pages of *Not Left Behind* was a beautiful Pit Bull whom I did leave behind. I purchased the book and openly cried in my car on the way home because I thought of the title of the book and then thought of Diesel along with all of the other dogs who I left behind in New Orleans.

I want to personally thank all of the rescuers who were on a mission to save the animals of New Orleans, something that I could not do during my two weeks of horror. They are the epitome of selflessness and I wish I could have saved those animals as well.

We currently have an all white American Bulldog, which we got when I returned from New Orleans. The vision of Diesel, who I thought was dead, was with me when we picked up our dog. I was hoping that you could tell me if you have found her a home. I would love to have her in my forever home if her disposition would allow her to bond to another female dog. If not, then I would love to hear if she has been placed into a loving home.

Thank you,
LTJG Brandon Guldseth
United States Coast Guard

It was a stunning letter, and it answered the questions we had about how Diesel came to be in the boat and who had painted those words, letting the rescue team know that a dog was hiding there. Her owner had not left her, as we'd originally thought, and her person had not painted those words on the side of the boat. Instead, it appeared she had taken cover in the boat, albeit next to a leaky diesel outboard motor.

In a telephone interview afterward, Brandon said it took him more than a year to adjust after he left New Orleans. "I was in a daze when I returned, not only because of what I saw," he said, "but because of what I heard and smelled as well. I think it took me over a year to process all the information, which bombarded my senses. The suffering and death of people and animals most certainly had an effect on my psyche."

Brandon was told that Diesel had been fostered out to a volunteer a week after she was rescued. For Brandon, knowing that Diesel was rescued and later placed in a home lifted the weight he'd felt all those months after having to leave her. Diesel, as the book Brandon stumbled across had shown, was not left behind after all.

2

Poodle on a Rooftop

WILLIAM MORGAN SAT STOICALLY as an attorney pushed his wheelchair to the podium inside the Louisiana State Capitol, a historic building in Baton Rouge.

But another kind of history was being made that day. It was May 22, 2006, a Monday, nearly nine months after William had been evacuated from the floodwater at the edge of his rooftop. A Louisiana legislative panel was convening to look into the treatment of people's pets in the aftermath of Hurricane Katrina. Morgan LeFay, William's apricot Standard Poodle, was by his side as he testified about their experience.

Legislators listened to speaker after speaker plead their cases for the animals—including William Morgan, who told the story about how he came to lose his dog, his companion, during the storm. When William, an articulate, educated man, spoke about his ordeal, those listening in the gallery openly wept.

According to William, he had not meant to abandon Miss Morgan, as he calls his dog, who was just a little more than a year old when the hurricane hit. A double-amputee and a war veteran in his early seventies who had served in the armed forces in France, William floated to the ceiling of his home when the Seventeenth Street levee was breached. He tried to punch through the attic roof but failed. When he realized that time was running out, he dog-paddled to a window and was able to get it open. He went through it and then swam to the eave of the roof.

But when William heard his dog frantically splashing at the ceiling inside his home on Benefit Street near Franklin Avenue in East Orleans, he swam back for her. Together, they made their way to the roof's edge, because there wasn't anything else for them to hold on to. William pushed his dog out of the water and onto the roof. But he couldn't get enough leverage to pull himself onto it.

For the next fourteen hours, William stayed in the water with one arm held tightly around a tree limb and the other around his dog as the rain and storm water slapped at them and thrashed them about. Because the storm hit while he was still in bed, William had not had a chance to get dressed. He was naked as he fought to stay afloat while keeping his dog out of the water. "I kept lifting and pushing Miss Morgan back onto the roof," William said. "She kept sliding back into the water." He knew if he let her go, she would wash away. Once she realized, however, that she wouldn't slip if she moved a few steps higher toward the peak of the roof, that's where she stayed put, a few feet from William.

United States Coast Guard members arrived in a boat at William's house fourteen hours into his ordeal. "They threw me a rope," William said. "I put it around me."

Then he asked, "What about my dog?"

"We'll get your dog," they promised.

"I won't get in until you get my dog."

"We will," they said. "You need to get in first."

"But as soon as they pulled me onto the boat, they sped away without Miss Morgan," he said. They told him they weren't allowed to rescue pets.

As William was motored away from his home, all he could see was his dog's confused face. "She was crying, whining, and barking," William said. "Several blocks over I could still hear her. It was awful." He thought he'd never see Morgan LeFay again.

William was taken by helicopter to the New Orleans airport, where he was given a hospital gown to wear, although, he said, "It was open and my backside was exposed." A day later, a stranger gave him a T-shirt. Because no wheelchairs were available, he stayed on a gurney at the airport for a couple of days before he was flown to a veterans' hospital in Miami, Florida. After a story about William's evacuation appeared in the *Sun Sentinel,* a volunteer there began an online search for his dog. A description was also posted on a lost-animal Web site, which asked animal welfare groups to be on the lookout for "Miss Morgan LeFay," and gave her description as twenty inches high, fourteen to sixteen months old, and not wearing tags.

Because the Petfinder lost-and-found Web site at www.pet finder.org wasn't yet available for evacuees, the volunteer had no way of knowing that on September 11, twelve days after William was tricked into leaving Morgan LeFay behind, a Best Friends rapid response team had rescued the dog from her perch on the roof, where she was still standing as if she were waiting for William to return for her. On the water with the team that day was Associated Press photographer Rick Bowmer. The image of a thin Poodle standing precariously on the peak of a roof, surrounded by water and floating debris, moved across the national wire. When the team got closer, the Poodle slipped into the water and they lifted her onto a flat boat.

The same team stopped by the Jefferson Parish Animal Shelter on their way back to Camp Tylertown to pick up more displaced animals. In the shelter was another apricot Standard Poodle, this one with matted, overgrown fur. No one could tell she was a Poodle until the next morning when she was groomed, shaved down, and put into a ten-by-ten run with Morgan LeFay.

Meanwhile, the volunteer working on William's behalf sent e-mails to the different rescue groups in the area. One e-mail made it to Camp Tylertown. Because the two apricot-colored Poodles had been rescued the same day and kept in the same run, no one could tell them apart. It was left to William to identify which one of the look-alikes was his. So, two weeks after the match was made, both Poodles were driven by volunteers Catherine "Cat" Gabrel and Virginia Kilmer for a reunion at the Miami hospital where William was receiving long-term treatment for cuts, bruises, and diabetes complications. As the two dogs stepped into the car to leave Camp Tylertown, an Animal Planet crew was on hand to film the two Poodles, who by then had become quite attached to each other.

Once in Miami, with the camera crew capturing the moment, there was no doubt. The real Morgan LeFay walked right up to William. "It was a wonderful reunion," Cat said. "You couldn't help but cry."

After the tearful gathering, Morgan LeFay and the second Poodle, who was named Dalilah, were driven by Cat and Virginia to the same foster home in Florida. Morgan LeFay remained there until William was released from the hospital and settled into permanent housing. Dalilah stayed behind with her foster family.

Nine months later, over Easter weekend in 2006, foster mom Linda Walser drove Morgan LeFay nine hundred miles to her new home with William in Alexandria, Louisiana, where Miss Morgan has a fenced yard and a doggie door. Linda took along plenty of tennis balls because Morgan LeFay had gotten hooked on playing fetch in her foster home. As before, Morgan LeFay recognized William immediately and ran to him.

Once home, William saw a difference in his dog, who had been young and still puppylike before the storm. Before Katrina, "Miss Morgan was a bull in a china shop," he said. "Now, she's at home both inside and out.

"She goes in and out of the dog door, and she [still] enjoys chasing squirrels in the yard. I didn't realize how much I missed her until she got here. It's truly wonderful. It's the best Easter I've ever had in my life."

It was just a few days after William and Morgan LeFay were reunited that William traveled to the Louisiana capitol to testify and tell his story to the legislative panel convened in the aftermath of Hurricane Katrina. William's was the most compelling of all of the presentations, according to Russ Mead, general counsel for Best Friends, who also spoke on behalf of the animals left behind. Besides spectators, even members of the committee appeared visibly moved by William's harrowing story.

On June 15, 2006, the Louisiana Pet Evacuation Bill was passed on the Senate and House floors and all the committees in between, and then it headed to Governor Kathleen Blanco for her signature. Even though the bill had no financing behind it, Blanco signed it into law. It was passed because of pressure from lobbyists and victims like William Morgan, and, in large part, because of a last-minute letter-writing campaign intended to pressure the governor to sign it into law. In September 2006, California governor Arnold Schwarzenegger signed a disaster-planning bill requiring officials to consider the needs of household pets, service animals, and livestock in an emergency. Then, on October 6, President George W. Bush signed the federal PETS Act, which requires local and state emergency preparedness authorities to include in their disaster evacuation plans accommodations for household companions and service animals. In a nutshell, the PETS Act recognizes that separating a human rescue-and-relief effort from an animal rescue operation is no longer acceptable to the American public.

Back in Louisiana, whether state legislators were influenced by William Morgan's words or not, William drove home the point to lawmakers on that May afternoon: Never again should people be forced, during desperate circumstances, to leave their pets to fend for themselves.

3

The American Can Company

WHEN KIMBERLEE LAUER ARRIVED at Camp Tylertown about a week after the storm, it was for one purpose: to let rescuers know that dozens of pets were trapped inside loft-style apartments at the American Can Company complex in Mid-City.

Those stranded in the turn-of-the-century converted factory included Kimberlee's Himalayan cat, Mr. Jezebel, and other animals. Kimberlee and two friends had left their three cats in a fourth-floor apartment in the high-rise building on New Orleans Avenue overlooking Bayou St. John. The American Can Company was surrounded by a seemingly endless wasteland of toxic water with animals inside homes just hanging on. The building was touted as hurricane proof. "It's a hundred feet off the ground," said Kimberlee, who had moved to New Orleans three years earlier. The problem was, no one could get to it, except by boat, and then only if they could get past the police and National Guard checkpoints. In that regard, residents were locked out.

Kimberlee didn't even live in the building. She'd gone with Mr. Jezebel to a friend's apartment in the American Can to ride out the storm. "We were on the roof, and you could see the whole city," Kimberlee said. Because the hallways didn't have windows and were completely dark, "everybody walked their dogs on the roofs, which connected the buildings. There were about two hundred people in the buildings. There was a little water in the street, and we figured we could drive out the next day."

That was Monday. "The levee broke the next day, on Tuesday," she continued, "and we said, 'Oh, no. We're stuck.'"

The day after the levees broke, the water was rising at the Orleans Avenue entrance to the apartments. The cars on Toulouse Street, at another entrance to the complex, were submerged. Medics and National Guard officers evacuated patients from the hospital next door. Kimberlee and others looked down from the American Can roof and watched the evacuation. "The medics had to push the patients in wheelchairs and on gurneys through the standing water," she said. "It was difficult. The ground was uneven. The water was above the cars. We had two weeks' worth of food and water. We figured we'd stay there till it was gone."

After spending four days at the Can, Kimberlee and her friends Suzanne O'Neill and Cem Cakir, who had two cats between them, were ordered to evacuate by National Guard officers and were then taken by helicopter to the New Orleans airport, where they waited for a flight out. "When we got to the airport," she said, "we discovered that some people had been allowed to bring their pets, and we were so jealous and angry that we weren't allowed to take ours."

They thought about nothing but their cats—Mr. Jezebel, Boo, and Raja. Despite what Kimberlee described as disorganization and chaos at the airport, they were each given MREs (military Meals Ready to Eat), and the restrooms and air-conditioning worked.

They called friends who had been evacuated, too. "A friend's dogs were rescued by some Australian journalists, and another friend's cat was rescued by someone who rode his bicycle into the city and then treaded water for twelve blocks. All these stories made us happy and desperately jealous at the same time. We just felt so powerless.

"We posted our info on all the pet sites we could find," Kimberlee continued. "We even posted a reward on Craigslist, asking if someone could go into the Can and get the cats safely back to us."

A friend's father picked up the trio in Houston, where they were flown, and drove them to San Antonio. Suzanne, Boo's person, learned that Best Friends was running an animal rescue center.

"Suzanne suggested one of us go there and plant ourselves with the rescue group in the hope that making direct contact would give us a better shot," Kinberlee said. "So that's what we did. I volunteered to be the one to drive to Tylertown that day." From San Antonio, Kimberlee flew to Missouri to pick up her car from a tenant who had borrowed it to evacuate to Texas. Then Kimberlee headed for Tylertown, Mississippi. "I even picked up a stranded dog on the way, a Chow who was accepted at Tylertown."

Kimberlee arrived at Camp Tylertown and told Paul Berry and Russ Mead her story. She also went to work, helping at base camp. "Kimberlee was one of the first volunteers to arrive here," said Heidi Krupp with the St. Francis Sanctuary.

"Best Friends," Kimberlee said, "was our best hope, because at that time, as far as we knew, they were the only rescue operation going into the flooded areas of New Orleans."

Kimberlee's plan worked. A team, which included volunteer Ken Ray and Best Friends rapid response members Ethan Gurney and Jeff Popowich, decided to go to the American Can Company on September 9 to rescue at least two dozen pets trapped in the apartment complex. Back at base camp, Kimberlee called her friends—and some other residents she'd gotten numbers from— to let them know that a team was going to try to rescue their pets.

It wasn't easy getting there.

Because the complex was surrounded by water, there was no way to get close to it by car. The team took Interstate 10 to an off-ramp, and then got a boat into the water. Even so, it took a long time to reach the building. "The water wasn't all that deep, and we had a person we met along the way guiding us there," said rescuer Jeff Popowich. "We had to maneuver along the side of the road to keep in deeper water. And, of course, there were animals along the way and we were stopping and picking them up."

They came across an empty boat floating in the floodwater, which they towed behind them and used later to transport some of the crated animals. Before they reached the American Can, they came across a woman who had been wading in the water, also trying to make her way to the building. She had keys to some of the apartments, which she gave to the rescuers. She pointed out the way out to the Can and then waited for them to return. When they boated back to her, she recognized a black Lab puppy in the boat. The dog was named Beauty, and the woman said she could give the puppy to his family, because she was in contact with them. The team returned the keys, and the woman took the puppy.

"We took two boats with us that day to the American Can Company," said Ken Ray, who was with the team the first day. "There were two groups of us. We launched from the same place we had been launching from before. It took us about an hour and a half to get there, because there were a lot of downed wires, and the water had dropped a lot. That was the day we had to tote the boats one hundred fifty yards over land. We divided up and each took different floors."

Kimberlee had given them a list of apartment numbers where she knew pets had been left. "We had gone through a lot of the list," Ken said, "and we were just looking for notes on doors."

By that point, it was getting dark. Kimberlee had warned them that looters might be in the building, or at least nearby. The team ran out of time and daylight. They didn't make it to the fourth floor where Mr. Jezebel and Kimberlee's friends' cats were left. They headed back.

They ran into an island—what appeared to be a rise in the road—that was one hundred fifty yards long. "The boats were overloaded and had to be emptied to carry them over the rise in the road," Ken said.

First they emptied the boats, carried them over the patch of dry road, and lifted them back into the water. Then, one by one, they carried the animals to the boats and reloaded them to continue motoring back to the transport van.

"We had to backtrack about four blocks to cross over," Ken said.

As they got into the boats, "two Rottweilers on dry land came toward us," Ken said. "They were friendly and healthy. These were 125-pound dogs. Those boats only hold 725 pounds each. I started doing the math. With the dogs, Jeff, Ethan, and me in the boat, I said, 'This isn't good. We're at the limit. We'll sink.' The dogs looked as healthy as anything I'd seen down there, and they were friendly."

Jeff agreed. "One was friendlier and came up to us," he said. "We put him in the boat and called the other one. He wouldn't come to us." Ken, who owned one of the boats, reminded them about the weight limit and the distance they still had to go to reach the van. "We put the other one back on the ground, because we didn't want the one to be alone," Jeff said.

They still had a half mile to get to the trucks and vans when they heard a dog barking. They followed the sound to an apartment building. "I climbed up to the apartment and got him down from the second floor," Ken said. A young kitten was at the apartment, too. Ken retrieved the kitten, who was later named Hurricane and fostered out to volunteer Tracey Simmons.

That night, they got in late to base camp. When Kimberlee heard the van arrive and was told that Mr. Jezebel wasn't with the day's rescues, she was visibly upset. "We'll get him tomorrow," Jeff told her. "We're going back."

"After that first night when the rescue teams came back and told me that they couldn't get to our cats, I didn't call Suzanne," Kimberlee said. "We had an agreement that I wouldn't call her until I could see the three kitties for myself and make sure they got all three and they were definitely ours. The rescuers said they were going to try again the next day. I cried and said I really appreciated them going back." The team left at five o'clock the next morning.

That second day, Kimberlee said, was especially difficult, because of the conditions in the city. She was worried they wouldn't be able to reach the American Can Company building a second time.

"I had that sick feeling in my gut," Kimberlee said, "and I couldn't get over it. I spent the day with the kitties who had already been rescued and tried to hope for the best. I heard the rescue van come in that night, and I just couldn't get out of my tent. I was sitting with Misha, a white Husky. She was my little guardian angel, and she comforted me the whole time I was there." (Misha's owner was located, but he was stuck in Texas with no transportation and no money. Weeks later, he borrowed a car and drove to Mississippi. But on that particular night, Misha kept Kimberlee company. Misha was kept tied out on a long cable because she didn't do well in the ten-by-ten-foot runs and she cried a lot. She was moved to the courtyard area at Camp Tylertown in front of the buildings, where she got regular attention. Ethan Gurney, a dog caregiver and a rapid response worker, sometimes slept on the grass with Misha, and they kept each other company.)

After a few minutes, Kimberlee left her tent and headed for the transport van. Included with the rescued that day were a small green parrot and three turtles. When Jeff told Kimberlee, "We got your cat," she broke down. They carried the crates into Kitty City so they could take the cats out. As Kimberlee opened the crate and picked up Mr. Jezebel, she said, "I never thought I'd see him again." Just then, he scratched her face. "He's mad at me for leaving him," Kimberlee said. "He's never like this." She called her friends Cem and Suzanne, who immediately drove to Camp Tylertown to pick up Boo and Raja.

Kimberlee lived in a condominium and owned a Laundromat nearby in the Garden District. Ironically, her house didn't flood like the Can did. "If I'd stayed there, I would have been fine," she said. Still, if she'd stayed at her condo, the Best Friends team might not have been notified about the urgency of the animals stranded inside the American Can.

"I was with Best Friends for a week before they were able to get into the Can," Kimberlee said. "I was devastated but trying to stay positive. The second rescue attempt was successful, and I got my baby back. It was such a huge relief. I felt as though I could finally begin to deal with what had happened to us. All I could focus on was how to get them all out. Once they were out, I felt like I could breathe again and start to pull my life together."

Connie Bordeaux, another American Can Company resident, left her Boxer puppy, Honey, and her two cats, Rusty and Feather, in a fifth-floor apartment. After she was forced to evacuate, she, too, began sending e-mails and calling rescue groups, asking if someone could go to her apartment and break in to rescue them. Honey and Rusty, a Himalayan cat, were rescued. The team didn't find Feather, a red tabby, despite looking under furniture for her.

Scott Biggerstaff's two dogs, Cobi and Bella, were left at the American Can building, too, but he didn't immediately know that. When Scott arrived at Camp Tylertown on a late September evening, it was with hope. When Hurricane Katrina hit, he and his wife, Teresa, were out of town. In their absence, Scott left Cobi and Bella with a friend, a doctor who lived at the American Can. When their friend evacuated to a hospital, he left the dogs in his apartment. After they began a search for their dogs, the Biggerstaffs learned that the first floor of the apartment building was flooded and no one was allowed into the area. They didn't know whether their dogs were still alive. They went to the Lamar-Dixon shelter in Gonzales, where nearly two thousand dogs and cats were already being housed. The numbers of homeless animals were so overwhelming that Scott and Teresa resigned themselves to never being able to find their pets.

When they got word from another friend who was able to get into the American Can that Best Friends rescuers had been there, the Biggerstaffs were hopeful. Scott called the Best Friends sanctuary in Kanab, Utah, and left a message. A couple of days later, he received a call back from Best Friends staffer Jill Dennis, telling him that Best Friends had his dogs. Scott got in his car and headed for Camp Tylertown.

When he arrived, the sun was just setting. I walked with him to a ten-by-ten-foot run where Cobi and Bella had been staying. When he walked in front of their run, the dogs had about a five-second delay before they realized who he was. They started barking at him and jumping at the fence, ecstatic to see him. Scott got in his car and drove them back to Charlotte, North Carolina, where he and his wife had relocated.

Later that day, September 16, six more people were reunited with their dogs and cats—most of whom had been rescued from the American Can Company apartments a few days before. The reunions included a Great Dane and a Catahoula.

Two cats retrieved during the two-day American Can rescue were Cici and Fifi, a tortoiseshell and a red tabby cat. Their owner had taped a letter for rescuers onto the apartment door. It was written as if it were from her cats, and it got the cats home. Here's the text of the note, dated September 1:

> Our names are Fifi and Cici. We are both cats, one boy, one girl. Please take us to a shelter. Our doctors are located at the Cat Practice.
>
> If you find us, we are in the restroom. We have enough food to last us 5 days.
>
> Please contact our parents, Daryl and Tasha, who love and adore us very much, at [and the phone numbers were given].
>
> Please, we need your help!
>
> Thank you, Tasha.

It was the day before the storm when Latasha (Tasha) Ratleff and her fiancé, Daryl Odom, a New Orleans police officer, took their cats to her grandmother's loft apartment at the former American Can Company warehouse. "The building was made to last through a Level 5 hurricane," Tasha said, "so we stayed there and rode it out." Then, at four in the morning on September 1, National Guard officers knocked on their door and told them they were being evacuated and that they had thirty minutes to pack up their things and leave.

"They said we could only take one bag and no pets," Tasha said. She was shocked and didn't know what to do about her cats. Daryl suggested she write a note about the cats with information on how to get in touch with her and leave it for rescuers to find. Tasha sat down, wrote the note, and taped it to the apartment door, hoping someone would find it.

Her note was found by rescuers Ken and Jeff, and Fifi and Cici were picked up during the team's first run to the apartment building on September 9. The problem for Tasha was that she didn't know about the rescue for a while.

Ken went into the apartment where Tasha had left her cats. "I went in with Jeff, and we got Fifi and Cici," Ken said. "The note was on the exterior door. I broke down that door. It got kind of chaotic at that point. The sun was starting to go down. One of those cats got Jeff pretty good when we got them from the bathroom. And, man, that bathroom reeked. The urine smell about took our breath away when we opened the door."

"It was hell," Jeff said. "The urine was so concentrated in there, it had turned to ammonia. It was nasty. And those cats were freaked out. I got one of them and caught the second. He was so freaked out, he got away from me. We caught him again in the bathroom, but it took a little while." He said a little bit of food was still left in the tub.

When Fifi and Cici arrived at Camp Tylertown, Tasha's note was put with a stack of intake papers completed by the rescue team who had found the cats that day. But Tasha's message wasn't discovered again until a week later when I was thumbing through the stack looking for a pet record. Sean Scherer, a twenty-year-old volunteer from Utah who is a whiz with computers, got into the center's database and began searching for any information in the records that even remotely matched information in the note. By then, there were one hundred fifty cats at the center. Sean found two cats, one a tortoiseshell and the other an orange tabby, who appeared to be Cici and Fifi. We went into the cattery looking for them and found Fifi. Tasha's other cat had been fostered out, so we made a note to call first thing in the morning and make arrangements to have Cici brought back to Tylertown.

By the time Sean found the cats in the database, it was eleven at night in New Orleans. Should workers try the phone numbers on the note and let Tasha know right away that her cats were fine, or wait until morning?

"Absolutely, call right now," somebody said. "She'll want to know. Her cats are like her children. You can tell by the note." When Tasha was told that Fifi and Cici had been rescued and that her note had been found, there was silence on the other end of the phone. Then she started to cry. "It's my birthday," Tasha said through tears. "It couldn't be a more perfect gift. Thank you. Thank you so much."

The reunion coincided with the couple moving into a new apartment (one that allowed cats) in the Uptown section of New Orleans. When Tasha and Daryl picked up Fifi and Cici a few days later, the reunions marked the ninety-ninth and one-hundredth pets returned to their owners from the Best Friends rescues, just three weeks after the storm. "You have no idea how important it is to get something this precious back," Tasha said that day. "You've given me my life back."

Daryl's reaction to the return of Tasha's cats was a simple "I told you so." She said he'd told her when they were forced to leave not to worry about the cats. As the couple stood on the Camp Tylertown grounds, each holding a cat carrier, Tasha remembered the conversation she and Daryl had had in her grandmother's American Can apartment just before they were evacuated. "He told me if I wrote a note, I'd get my cats back. He was right."

Mia, an eight-pound Chihuahua, was also rescued from the American Can Company, from a patio deck. Mia, who was seen swimming in four and a half feet of water with two other Chihuahuas, wasn't about to be plucked from the water, no matter how scared she was. Ethan Gurney saw her and waded in the water to get all three Chihuahuas. He walked onto the water-covered deck, following the dogs. However, what Ethan hadn't realized was that, because the four-foot-deep water was black and he couldn't see below the surface, he was walking on the deck of a swimming pool. When he took another step forward, reaching out to grab Mia, Ethan went underwater. Meanwhile, Mia kept swimming with the other two dogs. It was the end of the first day at the American Can; the rescue team had filled the boats to capacity, and they needed to leave. They returned to Camp Tylertown without Mia and the other Chihuahuas.

The next day they found Mia huddled in a recess of the building with just one other Chihuahua. As Jeff Popowich grabbed Mia this time, she bit at his hands. He held on and retrieved the other Chihuahua, too.

When the team arrived at Tylertown with the load of pets that day, a volunteer walked up to me and asked if I could keep one of the Chihuahuas, the little red one, with me for the day, because she was shivering with fright. She said she'd be back for her at the end of the day. The volunteer never returned, so I named the dog Mia (for Missing in Action) and kept her with me the rest of that first tour, about two months. Mia, who was listed on Petfinder but was never reunited with her person, and Lois Lane became best buddies.

4

Base Camp

W HEN HURRICANE KATRINA MADE LANDFALL in southeast Louisiana, residents of Mississippi, located in the heart of the South and one of five states bordering the Gulf of Mexico, were hit as well. The St. Francis Animal Sanctuary in Tylertown, located midway between Jackson, Mississippi, and New Orleans, was difficult to get to because of washed-out roads, downed power lines, and fallen trees on the streets leading to the sanctuary in rural Mississippi.

On Thursday, September 2, Paul Berry made it to the animal sanctuary after workers in a power company truck gave him a detour to follow. After spending a couple of days in New Orleans, he knew the storm was not a run-of-the-mill hurricane. When Paul finally realized through radio reports that officials were going to let the city flood and then try to fix the levees after the flooding had stabilized, he knew that it was a major catastrophe and that houses would be underwater. And he knew from growing up there that most people don't evacuate, and a lot of those people who stay behind have pets. While in New Orleans, he saw animals running all over the place, almost as if they were fleeing a tornado. They were, in fact, fleeing the rising floodwaters.

Ethan Gurney, Jeff Popowich, and Russ Mead, the first Best Friends team on the ground, arrived at the St. Francis Sanctuary on Sunday, September 5. On Monday, they started building runs with fences as a way to house animals from Franklinton, Louisiana, about twenty miles away, where the Jefferson Parish shelter had evacuated pets. With the help of TV and radio reports in Jackson, 80 of those dogs and cats were eventually adopted out, and through an agreement between the shelter (headed by Bert Smith) and Paul Berry at Best Friends, the Jefferson Parish shelter's remaining 110 pets were given to Best Friends to care for.

The agreement also called for Best Friends to care for, house, reunite, or foster out the animals to clear space for more Katrina pets at the Jefferson Parish shelter. That agreement was a pivotal moment in the rescue effort. As it turned out, the agreement not only was a way to help pets at the Jefferson Parish shelter, but also provided the permission Best Friends rescue teams needed to enter the city and get past military and police roadblocks along the way. With a copy of the signed agreement from Bert in hand each day, Best Friends teams were waved on past the half-dozen checkpoints while others were not allowed in.

In the meantime, back at the command center at the Best Friends sanctuary in southern Utah, phones were ringing off the hook.

"Calls to Best Friends began immediately when news of the flooding hit," said Anne Mejia, a Best Friends founder who directed operations at the command center. "Calls were overwhelming the switchboard."

It was the same for the Web site. "Within ten days, we received seventy-six thousand e-mails, and it shut down our Web site," Anne said. Lynn Tharp, a Best Friends employee who works at the sanctuary's welcome center, was one of those who transcribed messages. She and others worked seven-day weeks to handle the onslaught. "I lifted the messages from voice mail and wrote them all down," she said. "Other workers would then grab my notes and call or e-mail people back. You know how people wonder when they leave a voice message whether anyone listens to it? Well, I did. I wrote down each and every one of those messages. They followed a pattern: they either called to donate supplies, they wanted to volunteer, or they wanted us to get their animals out of their houses." Everybody, she said, was contacted, either by telephone or e-mail.

One such message, in a list sent daily to the Camp Tylertown rescue team, notified them that two cats, Blackjack and Baby Kitty, were left on the second floor of a house when the owner evacuated to Florida. Those two cats were so frightened, the owner said, that she wasn't able to round them up before she left. Her house was locked and the windows boarded. Her other four cats, however, evacuated with her.

As the Best Friends team and St. Francis employees organized and staged the base camp, volunteers began to show up. Within days, as word got out, they arrived in droves. Where one day only a skeleton crew was working, the next day it was a mini-city. Each night, a bullhorn sounded to announce the arrival of the day's transport van. On cue, forty to sixty workers headed out on foot for Ellis Island—so named for new arrivals—to welcome the day's animals from New Orleans. The incoming dogs, cats, and miscellaneous pets were given water and small amounts of food (to allow their systems to adjust to food again) and were put in their kennels until morning.

The volunteers who arrived daily "were amazing, both at the command center and at Tylertown," said Anne Mejia, who ran the command center in Utah. "People arrived every day from all over the U.S. and Canada. They ended up staying longer than they had planned, and when they called their bosses to get permission to stay longer, often their companies would say, 'Stay as long as you need, and we will pay you to be there. It's our way of helping.' We were blessed with veterinarians, dog trainers, groomers, firefighters, nurses, teachers, computer technicians, mothers, retirees, corporate executives, students, construction workers, artists, and so many other gifted and amazing people."

If people couldn't be on the ground, they helped in other ways. "There were animal welfare and rescue organizations from cities around the country that sent supplies—depleting their own resources—in order to meet our urgent needs," Anne said.

"They were delivered by their own volunteers, who stayed and helped. Along with other valuable items, they would lend us their spay-and-neuter mobile units and donate endless amounts of medical supplies." The individuals and organizations "never looked for any recognition," she said. "They were truly responding from their hearts. Volunteers and staff immersed themselves totally in whatever they were doing, owning their job with a fierceness."

And everyone worked together. "The bonds built out of respect and appreciation between people from such diverse backgrounds are forever with all of us," Anne said. "I will always be immensely thankful to all the organizations and individuals who gave so enormously from their hearts and saved so many lives. They are in my heart forever."

One of those groups was the Colorado Humane Society. Volunteers with the group arrived early in the rescue effort in a large cargo van that was equipped with built-in kennels, and they allowed a team to drive it into New Orleans each day to transport those rescued back to camp. The large transport van—which was in pretty good shape when it arrived—was an integral part of the daily rescues. It didn't take long, however, for the gray-and-black sludge and, later, toxic clay to coat the floor—and everything else inside and out. As a result, volunteers started referring to the van as "the Big Nasty." The name stuck, and before long, that was what the van was officially called. A caravan of trucks and a smaller van, with the Big Nasty usually in the middle, would leave each morning with empty crates and then return to base camp each night with a full load of anywhere from forty to eighty animals.

The next morning, dogs were examined by vets and then vaccinated, bathed, groomed, and placed in ten-by-ten grassy runs. Injured and sick animals were carried to a triage center set up in a bungalow with a tacked-on cardboard sign that read "M*A*S*H Unit." Cats were placed in kennels lined with baby blankets in a cattery called the TLC Cat Club or in a converted milking barn dubbed the Cat Barn. In the cattery, some of the felines roamed free, interacting with both volunteers and one another. Two of the walls were screened in, making it a partial patio so they could get fresh air and exercise.

Some dogs were walked into Pit Alley (which was later renamed Pooch Alley), where the Pit Bulls and Pit Bull mixes lived. Down the road from there, at the far end of camp, was the Back Forty for the larger dogs, like Mastiffs, Chows, Great Danes, Labs, and Rottweilers. Across from Pit Alley was the Romper Room (sometimes called the Bowery) for medium-sized dogs such as Beagles, hounds, and many of the mutts. Another area of runs, called Midtown, was for mama dogs and their pups. The smallest of the dogs, mostly Poodles, Chihuahuas, Pomeranians, Yorkshire Terriers, and Dachshunds of fifteen pounds and under, were housed in an area named Toytown (also referred to as Toy Story or Toyland). A watchman at the front gate of the forty-eight-acre property sat under a tarp at a table called the Kool-Aid Stand.

Next to Toytown was a cooling station for the small dogs. The larger dogs all had kiddy pools in their runs, plus caregivers sprayed down the dogs a couple of times a day to lower their temperatures in those hot late-summer days. Volunteers kept busy watching over the toy dogs to make sure they didn't overheat. Donated fans were also set up outside and aimed at the runs. The dogs who showed signs of too much heat were put in the bottom half of a plastic crate filled with a few inches of water to cool them down.

When people reuniting with their pets arrived at base camp and did not have basic supplies for their animals, volunteers would send them home with armloads of food and water bowls, kibble, leashes, shampoo, toothpaste, and whatever else they needed.

In one case, a seventeen-year-old who was with his mother walked barefoot onto the base camp grounds. Kit Boggio, a volunteer coordinator, asked where his shoes were. "I lost them in the water," he said. She asked what size he wore and then hurried over to one of the eighteen-wheelers loaded with supplies. She returned with a pair of size-eleven tennis shoes. "We can't accept these," his mother said.

"Yes, you can," I told the teen's mother. "They're a gift. America sent them."

America sent a lot—hundreds of boxes with tens of thousands of various supplies to help run the center. "Generous people from all over the country keep sending supplies for animals and people," said Faith Maloney, a Best Friends founder, after she visited base camp.

While everyone believed the public would be generous, the donations that poured in were overwhelmingly so. Leigh and Terry Breland, who live in Terry, Mississippi, fifteen miles southwest of Jackson, volunteered the use of their two-car garage as a central receiving spot for supplies. It wasn't until the eighteen-wheeler trucks began rolling down their driveway on rural Misty Lane, with its expansive lawns and ponds, that the Brelands realized just how generous Americans could be. They became instant warehouse supervisors as they took in and disbursed supplies.

"The day after a notice went up on the Best Friends Web site, we got a few boxes," Leigh said. "We thought that was going to be it . . . that we'd get some boxes in. Two days later, the trucks started coming, and they kept coming in. The people who sent supplies also sent letters and pictures. My mom [Joy Woods] made two scrapbooks of the letters. The outpouring of love and compassion from the country—from a little old lady who sent a collar from her deceased dog to children who sent a roll of paper towels with a drawing and a note—was unbelievable. It was emotional reading them. I'm still thankful for the opportunity. It changed our lives. It made us more focused on people, to be more kind and compassionate to those who can't help themselves, and to be more aware of people's feelings."

Back at Camp Tylertown, the rescue effort was just as intense. Donors had also shipped supplies there, and boxes were stacked before workers had a chance to go through them. Dog and cat food was placed in an open truck container for easy access.

Next to a mess hall area—where a tent was later erected—were rows of shelving in an L shape, loaded with donated supplies. It was Best Friends founder and director Francis Battista, during his stint as base camp manager, who organized volunteers to empty and inventory hundreds of boxes loaded with donated supplies. The end result was what everyone referred to as the Dollar Store, because it was for volunteers to grab for free whatever they needed, including shampoo, toothbrushes, bath soap, razors, batteries, flashlights, gloves, towels, and blankets—all items sent to the center by generous people throughout the nation. Separate shelving, in an area next to the Dollar Store, was set up for donated pet supplies, including leashes, collars, harnesses, food bowls, bedding, toys, T-shirts, and sweaters (which came in handy for the dogs in mid-October, as the weather cooled).

In addition, accommodations were there not only for Best Friends staffers but also for volunteers. Behind Ellis Island were three new temporary fiberglass showers, complete with hot water and tarps that substituted as shower curtains, built by photographer Clay Myers, Best Friends employee Andrew Ireland, and volunteer Doug Klein, a contractor from St. Louis. Across from the showers was a row of seven portable toilets that were emptied every day by a maintenance company. It was indeed a mini-city, albeit in a rustic environment, with all the necessary amenities for pets and people. Volunteers worked tirelessly from dawn to dusk feeding, watering, walking, and medically treating roughly four hundred dogs and two hundred fifty cats on any given day. But at the end of the day, volunteers could take hot showers.

Sherry Woodard, an animal expert who arrived at Camp Tylertown on the night of September 11, didn't know what she'd be waking up to the next day. "As the sun came up in the morning," she said, "I started looking around at all the animals, roughly two hundred fifty dogs and two hundred fifty cats. I've met all types of animals—lizards, snakes, ducks, pigs—but just in sheer numbers, it was extreme."

As kennel manager at the site, Sherry oversaw animal care. The first thing she did was separate the boys from the girls, and then, as she said, "figured out how to get all the animals in the shade."

She gathered up tarps, put in a request via the Internet for more, and had volunteers begin tying the blue plastic-covered canvas tarps along the sunniest sides and over the tops of each ten-by-ten dog run. Once finished, the runs ended up looking similar to the FEMA blue-roofed buildings seen throughout New Orleans—a temporary fix for the damage.

During the week of September 21, kiddy pools arrived for the dogs to cool down and splash in. "The dogs are having a blast," one volunteer commented as she watched them play. In the late afternoons, the dogs seemed to get their second wind. This is the time of day that photographers call the "golden hour" or the "gloaming," when the lighting is perfect. Cinematographers refer to it as the "magic hour," when life feels momentarily suspended in time. It is the hour just before sunset, between twilight and dusk, when the world is golden with light and shadows. At camp, that was when the animals came to life, when they tossed their toys in the air, chased each other, and wrestled. Dogs and cats awakened from their afternoon naps just before the sun began to set, when the air was cooler, and all they wanted to do was play. It was the gloaming of Tylertown. This rural, grassy, wooded property was operating in emergency mode. Yet there were short but memorable breaks from the frenzy during the late-afternoon hour.

At the end of the daytime shift, just before dinner, caregivers were relieved from their daily chores of feeding, watering, poop-scooping, and running dogs to and from the triage area. During this brief downtime, they often joined the canines in their runs to play ball or simply sit and watch them enjoy themselves. During one afternoon walk around the grounds, I saw a large run filled with Beagles become a playground of activity, with the dogs wrestling in the grass and jumping on top of hay bales left for them to play on. They also played hide-and-seek behind the haystack. On one particular day, in nearby Pooch Alley, a Pit Bull jumped around and splashed in a kiddy pool, not minding that she was in a run by herself. That same day in Toytown, two small terrier mixes wrestled on the grass, rolling around as one.

Although no rescue group was perfect in the chaos left in Katrina's wake, Best Friends appeared to be the only organization that kept track of the animals through a paper trail that enabled them to be traced. By the end of the second week, the system was in place and the movement of the animals could be followed. Katherine Glover and her husband, Rob Robison, had set up a similar system during Hurricane Andrew for another animal welfare group. This time they chose to volunteer their assistance at Camp Tylertown because, as Katherine said, "We liked Best Friends' emphasis on reuniting animals with their owners, which is not always the case with other animal groups."

It's a system that, when implemented, is foolproof. Each animal arriving at the center is assigned an ID number, which is etched on an aluminum tag and attached to the collar. Admissions photos are taken and uploaded to a database and to the Petfinder Web site; a copy is attached to the medical and admissions sheets. One copy of the paperwork is kept with the animals, following them wherever they go, whether it is to a different run or to a foster home.

Included in the paperwork were existing and new microchip numbers, because all dogs and cats at Camp Tylertown were injected with a microchip. Although the chips didn't help the pets during the Katrina disaster, they will make it easier to get animals home the next time. The chips, injected between the shoulder blades, contain individual identification numbers that are readable with an electronic scanner.

Dan Knox, with AVID microchip company based in California, traveled to shelters in Mississippi, Louisiana, and

Texas to inject animals and teach caregivers how to safely implant chips. A few days earlier, he'd been in the Belle Chasse area of New Orleans. "We talked to a veterinarian there," Dan said. "But we couldn't even get in," due to the flooding. That vet was housing two hundred animals. "We had to send chips to a nearby town, and the National Guard transported the chips for us."

Microchipping, Dan said, is a major key to getting pets home if they're lost again. With that in mind, on September 20, along with animal expert Sherry Woodard and a couple of volunteers, Dan organized a mobile microchip cart and went from kennel to kennel microchipping the pets at the Tylertown base camp. "Our goal is to get every pet here microchipped and scanned," Dan said at the time. The day before, with an electronic device that reads chips, the team scanned 50 percent of the pets to see whether any were already chipped.

Most of the canines, he said, "are friendly, tail-wagging dogs and were obviously well loved." And they'll now have microchips to help get them home.

Despite the paper trail and microchips, occasional accidents happened, but none that couldn't be rectified. In late October 2005, a month and a half after Best Friends' emergency base camp was erected, several rumors began circulating on blogs and in e-mails that people involved in local dogfighting rings were stealing Pit Bulls from Camp Tylertown. Best Friends, in turn, issued a notice on its Web site addressing the rumors. While no Pit Bulls were stolen, the posting did mention that two dogs were missing: one was loose on the St. Francis Sanctuary grounds (and later retrieved) and the other taken by an overzealous volunteer who, on the premise that he was taking her for a walk, actually took her home. In the latter case, a whistleblower, after reading about the missing six-pound Chihuahua, called Camp Tylertown to tell workers where Ginger was and who she was with. The good Samaritan had met Ginger a few days earlier and had asked the volunteer if he'd adopted her from Camp Tylertown, because she knew he'd been there. "They'll never miss her" was his response. She knew then that the Chihuahua had been taken without permission, and she notified Camp Tylertown.

Ginger was, in fact, very much missed. When a volunteer working in Toytown that morning realized the man had not returned Ginger, she alerted the kennel manager. Word spread, and it sent a wave of sadness across the camp, knowing that a tiny, shy Katrina refugee, who had already been through so much, was gone. No one knew then whether the man who took her wanted to breed her or simply give her a home. As it turned out, it was the latter, but volunteers didn't know that for weeks.

Once he was contacted and asked to return the dog, he willingly drove Ginger back to the rescue center, six weeks after she was removed. Ginger was in good shape and appeared happy and well cared for. The person she'd been living with delivered her with her favorite treats, a sweater, a harness, and a matching leash and collar. After he left the office, Ginger wouldn't take her eyes off the door, waiting for him to return. A manager at Camp Tylertown was asked if maybe Ginger could stay with the man and his wife. "We can't reward bad behavior," the manager said. Ginger quickly bounced back. By the next morning, she was back to herself, playing with two other little ones in the office during the day and sleeping on the floor with me at night.

Then, on October 29, the TEARS Animal Rescue group of Birmingham, Alabama, volunteering at Camp Tylertown, fostered Ginger and drove her to Pam and Gene Smith, who were eagerly awaiting the arrival of the transport van that evening, thinking they'd be fostering a large dog. Instead, they took home Ginger. Because Ginger had been abandoned three weeks before the storm in the front yard of a vacant trailer with twenty other dogs (the same yard as my Chihuahua foster, Lois Lane), the Smiths were allowed to adopt her. "She now has her own little-size toys, brings them from her bed to the den, and puts them on her blanket on the couch," Pam said. The family's other dog, a mutt named Roxy, "has always been a big toy lover, shaking them and playing catch with them. Now Ginger does the same. It's so funny to see a six-pound dog shake some of those bigger toys."

After Ginger was taken, Sherry Woodard, with a group of volunteers she'd enlisted, moved the runs for the small dogs at Camp Tylertown to an area directly in front of St. Francis's main building to make sure that no other little ones disappeared.

While Ginger may have been one of the smallest canines at Camp Tylertown, the tiniest dog to pass through the gates was another Chihuahua, this one an aging female weighing just two and a half pounds. Her name was Itty Bitty, a snarling, growling, barking girl with only a few teeth—and she knew how to use them. Itty Bitty, who appeared to bite out of fear, arrived with an eye infection, a balding coat, and the saddest look on her tiny face.

After a week in the office, however, she perked up and nonstop barking began. She was so snappy sometimes that she would let only a couple of people put a collar and leash on her in preparation for her walks outside. If they weren't quick enough, she'd grab a finger with her two remaining front teeth, bite down, and hang on. Once Itty Bitty warmed up to people, she was fine and liked to be held, but if anyone went near her when she was on someone else's lap, she would snap at them.

For some reason that no one ever figured out, Itty Bitty particularly disliked Jeff Popowich, a vet tech, even though she had not spent a significant amount of time with him. If he was anywhere nearby when she was carried or walked, she morphed into a lunging, snapping creature from the netherworld who could be heard all around the yard. Once, Jeff walked over to her when she was in that mode and, with palm down, offered her his hand. She quickly grabbed a finger and bit down, and Jeff stood there without wincing—even though, as she hung on, it had to hurt. (I know, because she had also bitten me.) After a minute, when she didn't get a reaction from him, she let go.

Shirley Swift Vogel, a volunteer from Jackson, Maine, saw past Itty Bitty's tough exterior. On day seven of Shirley's stint, she spent half of it with Itty Bitty and said this dog was her favorite pet at Camp Tylertown. "When that little teacup was in my arms, I just held her," Shirley said. "As small as she is, she survived." But Shirley had other dogs at home and couldn't foster her. Itty Bitty's original person was never found, and because she was a difficult placement with her aggressive ways and could have been euthanized if placed in the wrong hands, it was decided she would have a better chance at getting an understanding guardian through the Best Friends sanctuary in Kanab, Utah, where a quieter atmosphere might also help calm her. Itty Bitty, however, had gotten quite a reputation at Camp Tylertown, and it was not easy to find a volunteer heading west who was willing to deliver her to Utah. Eventually, an employee leaving for the sanctuary agreed. So on October 9 everyone said goodbye, and Itty Bitty left for Utah. While she was being vaccinated and having a microchip injected, I held her. Itty Bitty was so humbled by the whole experience that she rested her head, for the first time, on my shoulder, and I hugged her back. It showed us all that, despite the drama, she had a sweet side.

Once in Utah with adoption coordinator Kristi Littrell, Itty Bitty was just as spunky. "Itty Bitty is very vocal and definitely has separation anxiety," Kristi said shortly after the tiny Chihuahua arrived at Best Friends' sanctuary. "She is more vocal than any dog I've ever had, I think, and definitely has the largest vocabulary. She makes sounds I've never heard coming out of a dog. She barks at my cats constantly and is forever chasing them." Still, Kristi said, Itty Bitty was entertaining. "We had an 'argument' over her sweater [needed for the cold temperature] for a few days. She kept taking it off, and I kept putting it on while she tried to nip me. I won."

In mid-December 2005, an understanding family in Salt Lake City who had another Chihuahua with a similar attitude fostered Itty Bitty and ultimately adopted her. Her family renamed her

Little Lottie. Her new guardian reported back that Itty Bitty was doing wonderfully and that the family loved what they described as "her little personality." Those of us who were familiar with Itty Bitty and her pesky personality breathed a sigh of relief.

For Ross Hartill, when life at camp became intense or when he'd seen too much, he'd spend time with a shy Husky mix named Hobo Mississippi. "My emotions were affected in many ways," said Ross, originally from Scotland and serving as a volunteer coordinator and dog caregiver at base camp. Seeing the dogs and cats arrive each day, wondering where their people were, seeing the pets distressed because of what they'd been through—all of this sometimes got to him and made him homesick for his own dogs, and for his girlfriend. "The task just felt endless," he said. "Those times were very difficult, and when I was feeling like that, I would, when possible, give myself a time-out and visit with Hobo."

As part of his responsibilities, he cared for the staff-only dogs, those with special issues who required experienced handlers. "The issues ranged from people aggression, dog aggression, medical needs, and escape artists." That's where he met Hobo.

"Hobo Mississippi had aggression issues with humans, and, as I'm human, he didn't give me any special treatment," he said. "When I say aggression issues, I mean growling, snarling, and snapping. As I would approach his run, he would growl and show signs of aggression, so I worked on him with treats through the fence."

Learning that Hobo was food-motivated helped Ross as he entered Hobo's run with a food bowl, keeping him busy as he quickly poop-scooped his run and refilled his water bowl. "With more than four hundred dogs at Tylertown," Ross said, "I don't know what it was that kept making me return to him, but we started to form a bond. I kept wishing that his people would one day come back to claim him, but that day never came. Every time I passed near his run I would call out his new name, and in a short time he stopped growling at me."

Hobo would stretch out, yawn, and look to Ross for treats. Still, Hobo wouldn't look him in the eye. It made Ross wonder if Hobo was frustrated about his situation, missing his people. "He was reluctant to look at me eye to eye, but he would rub up against the fence and allow me to touch him," he said.

Five months after Ross met Hobo Mississippi at base camp, the dog was driven to the Best Friends Utah sanctuary to live in an area called The Lodges in Dogtown, where the canines are housed. Once there, Ross said, "I'd still visit with Hobo, and he showed similar characteristics as when we first met."

One day, however, Ross decided to try something new. "As I walked up to his run, he greeted me with his usual barking until he recognized who I was. Then Hobo stretched out, yawned, and came to me looking for his treat."

After giving him treats, Ross made his move. "I entered his run, and he was pleased to see me—no fence and no growls. I asked him to sit for his treat, and he did."

He also tried handing him a toy, but Hobo Mississippi was unsure of what to do with it. Then, "as I left his run, he brushed up against the fence, wanting to be petted. Kneeling down to him, he pushed toward the fence, and as I rubbed his neck, he looked straight at me."

For the first time, Ross said, "I could see myself reflected in his eyes."

Ross, like so many other staffers and volunteers at base camp and in the field, had sought comfort—and had found it—from the very animals he was helping. It was truly a give-and-take between the rescuers and the rescued.

5

On the Ground

TWO WEEKS AFTER THE STORM, the search-and-rescue missions for all animal groups in the Gulf region was changing from a water operation to a massive ground operation. As the water receded each day from the streets of New Orleans, rescue teams switched from boat searches to land rescues. Teams were forced to shift gears and regroup as they continued saving as many animals as possible.

By mid to late September, as the high humidity and heat continued, time appeared to be running out, because no one expected many animals to survive more than a few weeks. Local officials finally allowed a Best Friends team into St. Bernard Parish, where it was known that thousands of animals were still alive and in desperate need of rescuing.

The pets were becoming tougher to catch. Instead of being approachable on the street, as many rescuers experienced in the early days of the rescue effort, animals were becoming street-savvy and semiferal. One Pit Bull mix, later named Bright Eyes, stood cowering—and cautious—behind a chain-link gate. As trapper Ethan Gurney approached, the dog showed his teeth and snarled, and started to actually scream with fright. "I've never heard a dog scream like that. I didn't think they could make that kind of noise," said Clay Myers, who photographed the rescue. Ethan was determined to pull him from the yard behind the vacant house, so he waited until Bright Eyes calmed down. Ethan knelt down and waited, talking softly to the dog. Using a catch pole, he was able to slip the noose around the dog's neck and slowly walk toward him to pet him, albeit with a padded-gloved hand. "Once Ethan put his hand out to him to pet him, he calmed down. That's when [the dog] stopped screaming," Clay said. The two walked side-by-side—with Bright Eyes still leashed by the pole—to the transport van, where he was given food and water and then taken to Camp Tylertown.

A similar scenario played out in Gentilly, in Orleans Parish, when Ethan helped catch a huge Rottweiler named Sheriff who was running loose on a street. Because Sheriff was wary of people, he, too, was rounded up using a humane catch pole and then taken to base camp. Today, Sheriff, who likes some people but can still be distrustful, resides at the Best Friends sanctuary in Utah, where he will live out his natural life.

But some pets were still friendly, making it easier for them to be rescued. For a family of three dogs, three cats, and a guinea pig from St. Bernard Parish, all but one dog, one cat, and the guinea pig made it home. "My husband, Preston, stayed behind," said Diane Bartholomew. "He put our pets on a flat boat. He had his boat tied to our magnolia tree, and that's where they rode out the storm. Rescuers came around in boats but didn't want to take the dogs."

Eventually, though, Preston was forced to leave. "He left our pets with a shrimper at the Violet Canal," she said.

Two of their cats scratched Diane's husband and wouldn't get in the boat, so he left them at the house. When the Bartholomews returned home the first week in October, the cats—Midnight and Sunny Boy—were still there. Two dogs, Chico and Duchess, were rescued by Best Friends near the shrimp factory, taken to Camp Tylertown, and then placed in foster homes. Chico was reunited with his family in December 2005, and Duchess a month later. "The shrimper got in touch with us four or five weeks later," Diane said. "Our dogs hung out at the old shrimp factory. People who worked there returned and fed them." Their third dog, Zeus, wasn't there, however; Diane said, he "might have wandered off." A third cat, Morning Star, and the guinea pig also have not been located.

To this day, in the evenings, Diane goes down to the shrimp factory on Pakenham Drive to look for Zeus. "I talk to people and show them photos," she said. "I ran into two people who thought they'd seen him. He's scared. He's a sweet dog, and we surely do miss him. My other two dogs are doing great. I kept the hope and prayed that they'd get back to me, and they did. I know how lucky I am to have them back. I surely do."

In addition to the base camp in Tylertown, other rescue groups were also taking in animals at temporary shelters set up at the Lamar-Dixon Exposition Center in Gonzales, Louisiana; the Parker Coliseum at Louisiana State University; the Mutt Shack shelter at Lake Castle School, across the road from Lake Pontchartrain, with no electricity or running water; Animal Rescue New Orleans on Magazine Street, which was set up in a former hair salon; a parking-lot shelter at a Winn-Dixie supermarket in Gentilly on Chef Menteur Highway; and the Humane Society of Louisiana, which set up at a neighboring site in Tylertown.

Most helicopter pilots and rescue boat captains were refusing to load people's pets because of the lack of space. In addition, those evacuating to the Superdome were banned from taking their pets with them. The staggering number of animals left behind was estimated to be in the tens of thousands. Pet owners were beside themselves, worrying about not only family members, but their pets, too.

But not all pets needed to be evacuated. Some stayed in their homes while volunteers stopped by periodically to care for them. This became the mission of Beth Montes, who runs one small cat sanctuary in Arizona and another in Missouri. By September 17, she was working from a list compiled daily by volunteers at the Best Friends command center in Utah. Evacuees called in, giving their addresses and the number of pets left in their homes. After volunteering at Camp Tylertown for two weeks, Beth left for New Orleans, despite people warning her of snipers and looters roaming the city throughout the night. She was determined to make a dent, no matter how small, in the list of people wanting someone to check on the welfare of their pets. From the field, she sent a few e-mails when she was able to get wireless Internet service. The following is a thumbnail view, from an e-mail, of her long days spent alone on the streets.

> I spent yesterday going door-to-door, working the list of animal locations. Some had gotten out, others I fed and watered and left notes on the doors. Residents are starting to come back in today, so I will check these animals again in three to four days, to make sure all now have people with them. I saw no sick or distressed animals, just hungry and thirsty ones.

Two crews of Buddhist monks had also gone into the city, Beth continued, "to some of the worst-hit areas, in the Gentilly area, between St. Charles Avenue and Milan Street."

But before going into that pocket of the city, the two teams of monks did a final sweep of the American Can Company building, the large apartment complex from which Best Friends had earlier rescued animals, to make sure no pets were still there. "When I last talked to the monks, they were nearly finished with that and had left food and water for some healthy animals who were safe in apartments," she wrote.

Beth emphasized her feeling that feeding and watering at that juncture for some neighborhoods was a good approach "rather than taking the animals out, since people will soon return [and] there is little space to house them in shelters or sanctuaries, and this avoids the chaos of trying to reunite them with their people."

The door-to-door home checks were an important step in the rescue operation. It meant that, even though the animals were not removed from their homes, they were being looked after, if only every few days, until their owners returned.

Her dispatch from the field explained her plans.

> I'm continuing with that effort today, here in Metairie. I'm currently planning to come back to St. Francis tonight, and will be

bringing one rescue dog that Virginia [Rankin, a St. Francis board member] picked up yesterday. She is definitely an owned animal, spayed, crate trained, collar hair loss, but no collar.

That dog was Zoey, whose nearly six-month journey began when Annie Johnson, her person, left her with a pet sitter in Metairie while Annie and her family went on vacation a week before the storm. The Johnsons' other dog, Muppie, stayed with a different sitter. When Katrina struck the coastal region, Zoey's sitter evacuated with her own dog, leaving Zoey by herself in the sitter's backyard, a neighborhood Zoey was unfamiliar with. In the sitter's defense, like so many other residents, she no doubt thought Zoey would be alone for just a couple of days. Once the storm subsided, the sitter would return for her. Instead, Zoey, like thousands of other pets, was left stranded.

Meanwhile, on day fifteen following the storm, Virginia Rankin, who'd evacuated with her family to their second home in Arkansas, got her daughter settled there and then headed to the Camp Tylertown hurricane relief center at the St. Francis Animal Sanctuary, for which Virginia is a board member.

After several days at base camp, Virginia decided to assess the damage to her Metairie house, which, as luck would have it, was just a mile and a half from where Zoey had been abandoned.

Although a tree had fallen on Virginia's home, it was livable and still had electricity and running water. A friend stopped by with rescue provisions, which they began moving into the house. United States National Guard officers stopped by to remind them there was still a six o'clock curfew in effect. After Virginia's friend left so he could get home before curfew, Virginia sat on her front porch. "My neighborhood was void of people. It was very eerie," she said.

All of a sudden, a German Shepherd mix bounded up to her like she was her long lost friend. It was Zoey. "I was very surprised to see her, but glad at the same time," Virginia said. "I grabbed her, brought her inside, and gave her the once-over. She wasn't injured that I could tell, and after a good meal and some water, she fell asleep on the rug in front of the TV."

The next day, Virginia toured the area with another friend, with Zoey in tow. As it was getting close to curfew again, they headed back to Virginia's house. On the way, they met Beth Montes. Few cars were in the area, so when they spotted each other's cars, they stopped to talk. They learned of each other's connections to Camp Tylertown and the St. Francis Sanctuary. When Beth told Virginia she planned to sleep in the van that night, Virginia wouldn't hear of it and invited Beth to stay with her. In exchange, Virginia asked if Beth could deliver Zoey to the sanctuary when she returned to Camp Tylertown the next day.

In the hubbub of activity, Zoey was accidentally sent not to the Camp Tylertown base camp but to the St. Francis Sanctuary on the same grounds, where she entered the general animal population without going through the admissions process for rescues. At St. Francis base camp, she was named Little Bit.

Meanwhile, Annie Johnson, Zoey's owner, did not learn until after two months had passed that Zoey was missing. Annie had tried during that time to phone Zoey's sitter, but her number had been disconnected, because most of the phone service in the area was still down. Annie assumed that Zoey was safe at the dog sitter's home or that she had evacuated the city with her. Annie finally reached her sitter and was amazed to learn that the sitter had taken her own dog but had left Zoey alone and unprotected outdoors in the yard during the hurricane. She further learned that the fence surrounding the sitter's yard had been washed away. Annie and her family were sick with worry.

Before the storm, Annie had taken Zoey to the vet to be treated for mange and heartworm. Knowing that Zoey had just undergone a tough medical treatment caused her more concern. She was worried that Zoey hadn't survived. Annie sent e-mails and fliers to the rescue groups in the area and did not lose hope of one day getting her dog back. Her family, she wrote, wouldn't be whole until they found their dog.

Months later, on the night of February 9, 2006, Heidi Krupp turned on her computer at the St. Francis Sanctuary and pulled up the Petfinder Web site, a national database with a lost-and-found section devoted to the animals of hurricanes Katrina and Rita.

"I sat down and went through some Petfinder photos of lost pets," Heidi said. "I absentmindedly clicked onto some photos, not paying a lot of attention." Then one photo suddenly jumped off the screen at her. "I said to myself, 'I think that's one of our dogs. That's Little Bit [Zoey].' I could hardly speak, I was so excited." From the contact information provided on Petfinder, she e-mailed Annie. "I told her I thought we had her dog," Heidi said. "I sent her a photo of the dog we had named Little Bit." When Virginia Rankin found out, she logged onto the Petfinder site and posted a reply to Annie's online note. It said: "[Zoey] is safe and was not injured during the storm. She was well behaved with her rescuer and has been well taken care of by the wonderful people of St. Francis." She included a phone number for the sanctuary.

Annie immediately called the number and reached Heidi. Her first question to her was, "Are you sure it's her?"

"I've never been more sure of anything in my life," Heidi told her. That's because, besides the online photo Annie had posted, all the identifiers—both physical and behavioral descriptions so important for making matches—fit perfectly: "cropped tail, heartworm positive, great with children, dogs, and cats, suffers from demodex mange, primary colors brown and black, spayed female."

"Annie cried and cried on the phone," Heidi said. "I told her, 'Don't cry. Zoey is fine. She's happy and living in a run with Buddy.' He's going to miss her. They play a lot."

Zoey had moved in with the Johnsons the year before the storm, after they rescued her from the street. At that time, in addition to having mange, Zoey appeared to have been in a dogfight. So Annie was especially relieved to hear that Zoey was safe and had survived hurricanes Katrina and Rita.

Pam Perez, cofounder of St. Francis with her daughter Heidi, drove Zoey home to Kansas, where the Johnson family had relocated. Zoey has settled in well with Annie's daughter Emma, their two cats, and their second dog Muppie. "I knew Little Bit was her dog Zoey," Heidi said.

Zoey wasn't the only dog left on the streets to fend for herself, out of no fault of her guardian. As the weeks passed and it became clear that thousands of pets—not just stray animals—had survived the storms and were now loose on the streets, a coalition of rescue groups went into a third phase of the rescue operation, which included setting up feeding stations, tracking, and trapping the pets humanely. By then, it was the end of November, and the pets had been without human companionship for three months.

The groups were heeding to what was considered a cry for help coming from the animals still on the streets after being left homeless when the storm swept through the region. Cats sat on porches and sidewalks, waiting. Dogs hid under houses and behind rubble. They migrated to where the food and water sources were, to the neighborhoods where residents were return-ing to clean up the debris. Animal rescuers, some of whom remained in the area, used traps (crates with a trap door) and poles to catch some of the frightened animals. Once they got to the rescue center, the pets eventually came around and started trusting people again.

An example of a feral-like refugee animal on the streets for months was Munchie, so named because he was a biter. Veteran animal trapper Corolla Fleeger, who spent six months in the Gulf catching animals, described Munchie as one of the toughest dogs she has met, and she has seen it all. An animal control officer in the Algiers community, on the west bank of the Mississippi River in Orleans Parish, caught Munchie, a fluffy red Pomeranian. From there he was taken to a shelter, where workers wrote on his kennel card that he was "very dangerous and will bite." Also on his paper-work it was noted, "Ill-advised to place this dog with a family." No one could get near Munchie, not even a vet to examine him. Corolla spent several weeks working with Munchie, sometimes just sitting next to his kennel, until he finally stopped trying to bite her.

When she began volunteering, Corolla said she was not adopting a Katrina animal. But with Munchie, it was different. When Corolla left New Orleans in early 2006, she took Munchie to live with her in Southern California. In April 2007, more than a year after he had moved in with her, Munchie's health gradually deteriorated. He had seizures every few hours and suffered from edema, plus luxating kneecaps so severe that he was unable to walk. Corolla said good-bye, and Munchie passed away in her loving home, not on the streets of New Orleans.

Munchie was an example of how frightened dogs and cats became in the months they spent without people around them. Once Corolla and others started working with lots of patience with animals like Munchie, they began to show progress.

Corolla was one of a track-and-trap team in the field. I followed her around for a day as she set traps and checked on animals she'd been tracking for days and, in some cases, weeks. Then, on January 4, 2006, Clay Myers and I left early in the morning for the Lower Ninth Ward to cover the work of two other volunteer trappers: Craig Hill, a self-employed gutter installer from South Brunswick, New Jersey, and Ann Welling, a student from Cincinnati, Ohio.

Later in the day, we drove to a street near a trap Craig had set in the middle of the night. Inside the trap was a black Pit Bull mix. Just as Craig was getting ready to load the dog into his van, an NBC affiliate, Channel 6 from New Orleans, drove up. They stopped to ask Craig what he was doing. A reporter interviewed him, even though Craig was hesitant and had never been on TV before. At four thirty in the afternoon, the reporter did a stand-up report, which was another vehicle on which animal welfare groups relied to get the word out to locals that people's pets were still wandering the streets or hiding under houses.

Of all the dogs and cats Craig rescued, only two captured his heart enough for him to adopt. One was a Vizsla mix who was found in a canal with obvious birdshot injuries across the side of her body and head. The prognosis wasn't good. On top of the shooting injuries, she was so frightened that it took three hours for a team to catch her.

Today, the only reminders of her time in the canal are a few scars. Her X-rays reveal far worse: more than a hundred pellets still imbedded under her skin, some in organs. Twelve remain in her left rear foot alone.

"They pierced every organ in her body but her heart," said Craig, who, along with nearly a dozen volunteers, rescued the dog he named Kanal Girl. Spray painted inside the canal where she lived with another dog for two months were the words "Kanal Boyz," probably the name of a street gang. "That's where she was hanging out, so that's why I spelled her name that way," he said. Craig adopted her "because she chose me. She follows me everywhere I go."

In early November, before Best Friends and Animal Rescue New Orleans set up a temporary triage center at Celebration Station in Metairie, Craig and his fellow rescuers had set out to capture Kanal Girl. "She was terrified," Craig explained. "She was scared and skinny. It took twelve of us three hours to get her. I jumped in the canal with fencing to block her." Still, she continued to run the length of the six-mile canal. "We walked three miles to get her. We started to sandwich her in, then she took a turn at the pump station." When she did that, they surrounded her and blocked her again. Finally, they were able to catch her and take her to a veterinary hospital in Metairie.

Prior to her rescue, she had been spotted by the Louisiana SPCA hanging out at the canal with a Chow who had been picked up earlier. Construction workers tipped off animal rescuers in the area that two dogs had been living in the canal for two months, and a resident regularly left them food.

"I was told the Chow was adopted by a family in New Jersey," Craig said. "When I get back home, I'm going to get together with them so Kanal Girl and the Chow can see each other again."

Craig remained in New Orleans until March 2006 after vowing to stay "until there aren't any more animals to pick up."

Animals weren't the only ones being picked up from houses. Volunteers sometimes came across unusual situations and had to make decisions on the spot. Such was the case when a team went into a storm-ravaged home to retrieve a cat. The only thing undamaged in the house was a dresser in the master bedroom. On it, unscathed and seemingly untouched, was a velvet-lined leather jewelry box. The volunteer was worried that looters who had been spotted in the area would take it. She searched the house and found a utility bill identifying the owner and walked out of the house with the bill and the case. Fellow rescuers carried the cat out of the house.

When the volunteer returned to base camp, she kept apologizing for taking the case, saying she hadn't known what to do, but she felt sure the owner would have wanted her to take it for safekeeping. Silva Battista (one of the founders of Best Friends with her husband, Francis, who were managing base camp at the time) took charge of the case, and I was tasked with notifying its owner. After some Internet searching, I reached the owner by phone to tell him that we had recovered not only his cat but also a jewelry case. A week or so later, he arrived at camp to pick up both. He thanked everyone for retrieving not only the family pet, but his wife's jewelry, too, commenting that heirlooms were in the case.

As time passed, it became more common to see a lone pet living in a neighborhood—or none at all. In Plaquemines Parish, where Susie Duttge (who fosters cats and helps strays near her home in Lake Bluff, Illinois) and photographer Clay Myers went looking for strays, a five-month-old kitten was the only pet still in the neighborhood. "She's my beautiful, strong-willed, soft-hearted girl," Susie said. "She was the only animal that survived in her neighborhood five and a half weeks after the storm."

Susie walked the abandoned, storm-destroyed neighborhood with Clay in early October. She had a feeling, a sense, that there was life in the neighborhood, even though there were no visible signs. The streets were deathly quiet, but then they heard a weak meow. Susie followed the sound until she came upon the house the meows were coming from. "We had no trap, and I knew I had only one chance to get her without one," Susie said. They lured the kitten out from under the house with food, and then Susie picked her up.

She sat on Susie's lap on the drive back to base camp. "When she wrapped her little paw over my finger and pulled it tight to her, that was it," she said. "I told her I would not leave her. I knew at that moment that I would bring her home with me."

At home in Illinois, the kitten, now called Nola Vie (*Nola*, from New Orleans, Louisiana—NO LA—and *vie*, which means "life" in French) is thriving since the ordeal of weathering a hurricane alone. "My other three cats let her rule the roost," Susie explained. "They've understood there's something different about her since the day she joined our home."

Nola Vie has a special talent, Susie said. "I toss these little play mice at her, and it doesn't matter if she's in front of me or down a hall in another room, in the dark, she jumps in the air, twists, and catches them. She'll weave in front of my feet until I throw the mice, one after another, every two seconds. She's just amazing."

She also does something that reminds Susie of the day she rescued her. "She's a very happy cat and still pulls my fingers to her as she did that day in the rescue truck. Every day that goes by, I think how lucky I am to have her."

While Nola Vie may have touched Susie's heart, it was a lone goose in St. Bernard Parish that brought Susie to tears. Volunteer Chipa Wolfe, who specializes in wildlife rescues, was with the team that day.

They stood quietly on a damaged corner just before sunset, knowing they needed to leave but still looking around for more animals. Martial law was in effect, and they needed to be out of the area before dark. "We heard the strangest noise come out of the eerie silence," Susie said. They looked around, and then they spotted her: a goose running toward them from behind her hiding place across the street, next to what remained of a corner market and a gas station.

"She was waddling as fast as she could from the side of the destroyed food mart, honking 'I hear you. I'm here, and I am alone. Don't leave me.'

"Chipa spoke so quietly and sweetly to her," Susie said. "He said, 'I love you. You deserve to live.' He carefully placed the net over her, and she didn't so much as flutter a wing. She just let it happen. That was part of the amazing beauty of that day."

Chipa picked up the bird in the net and sat her in the back of his covered pickup bed, where he released her beside loose dogs and crated cats they'd rescued earlier.

"The animals all got along," Susie said. "They knew they had been saved, and at that moment they all were on equal ground."

Back at camp, Susie couldn't shake the sight of the bird chasing after them. "I broke down, flooded with tears, in my tent at three in the morning, thinking of her plea and how desperate she was," Susie said. "It was the most gut-wrenching scene of all of my weeks down there. She truly was symbolic of all the lives we encountered and rescued."

6

Message in a Bottle

I'M GARY KARCHER, and this is Himie," begins a letter introducing a New Orleans dog to his potential rescuers. Writing the letter was a leap of faith for Gary, who in his note pleaded with rescuers for the safe return of Himie and also for the return of his mother's two dogs.

Gary's action that September day—armed with a pen that barely worked and a scrap of paper—was a clear example of the importance of using some sort of identification on pets, if only a note scrawled on scrap paper. For Himie and his housemates, Pudgy and Precious, the letter worked. Himie, a purebred Rottweiler, resembled every other Rottie who was rescued and taken to Camp Tylertown. Without the note, it's difficult to guess whether Gary would have been able to locate Himie. But because of the primitive note attached to Himie, the threesome was reunited with their family.

Himie's story began on a sultry afternoon, on the last Saturday of August 2005, when Gary Karcher sent his eighty-two-year-old mother out of New Orleans. "My mom evacuated with my sister and brother-in-law two days before the storm," Gary said. "She wanted to stay. I told her not to."

"What about the dogs?" Ethel Karcher asked her son.

"They'll be okay," he told her. "I'll stay with them."

And he did. A couple of days later when the levees broke, flooding St. Bernard Parish—one of the hardest-hit areas in New Orleans—water rushed into Gary's house. Within fifteen minutes, it was above the windows. For a week, he weathered the storm with Himie, along with Pudgy and Precious, his mother's Dachshunds.

"During the eye of the hurricane, that's when the water came up," Gary explained. Before he knew it, the level inside his home had reached four and a half feet. As the storm water rose even higher, he knew they needed to get outside; otherwise they would not make it. "The [windows] broke and the water rushed in even more," Gary said.

Once it leveled off, Gary called the dogs and "they came swimming to me." He lifted Precious and Pudgy onto the back of the sofa and commanded Himie to sit on the cushions. Then he tried to push, one by one, the dogs outside through a window, but they kept swimming back inside.

Finally, he grabbed a plastic trash can floating in the house, put Pudgy and Precious inside it, swam through a window opening, and pulled the trash can outside with him. "That trash can was their lifeboat," Gary said. Once he and the doxies were out of the house, Himie followed. "I put Himie on the roof of my station wagon and told him 'Stay.' When I rose up out of the water to push Himie onto the car, the wind blew the trash can, with Pudgy and Precious in it, toward my neighbor's fence. I followed it. I sat in the water and hung onto the fence with one hand and held the trash can with my other hand." It took four hours for the violent winds and surging waters to subside. Himie, Gary said, stayed "right there on the station wagon the whole time."

When the storm finally died down, a neighbor tied out a boat in Gary's backyard, and Gary coaxed Himie off the car and into the water. Gary waded in the water, still pulling Pudgy and Precious in the trash can, while Himie swam next to him. Then Gary pulled the dogs and his neighbor's dog, Rocky, onto the boat. "I told my neighbor, Rick, not to untie the boat, because we'd end up in the channel. But we were in the boat about an hour when the wind started to pick up and carry us away," he said. The two men got out of the boat and made their way to a nearby two-story house on the street behind theirs, pulling the boat beside them, with the dogs still inside. While Gary and Rick climbed through a second-floor window to safety, the dogs waited in the boat. They eventually maneuvered through the house to the first floor, and then waded back to the boat to retrieve the dogs. It took several hours to get everybody settled upstairs.

A day later, sheriff's deputies approached the house in a rescue boat and told Gary and Rick to get in with them. Gary politely refused, but his neighbor complied. The deputies would not let Rick take Rocky, a Labrador Retriever. "It's okay. Rocky can stay with me," Gary assured Rick. For several more days, Gary lived on the second floor with his dogs. At one point, he got back in the water and went home to retrieve Himie's eye salve from the medicine cabinet. Before the storm, he had been applying it because of an infection in Himie's left eye. On the way back from his house, deputies stopped Gary and told him again that he needed to get in their boat. He tried to reason with them: "I told them I had dogs I was taking care of. I wouldn't get in, and they told me they'd come and get me tomorrow with a gun."

Gary returned to the dogs and began hunting through the house for something to write with. He found a pen and a dry piece of notebook paper. He wanted to make sure that Himie had information with him, however primitive, that would help him get back home again. Otherwise, Gary knew he might not ever see him or his mother's dogs again. The following is the text of the letter Gary wrote in hopes his rescuers would read it.

HIMIE he's a big baby.

Hi I'm Gary Karcher, and this is Himie. He is two years old and has been on heartworm [prevention] meds for two years. He is well trained and loves kids and other dogs, and housed train.

I risked my life to save the three dogs, the other two are wiener dogs and they have been on heartworm med also.

I stayed with them high & dry for a week on a 2nd floor. The water went down to about 1-½ feet. I'll put all the water that is in the water heater in pans and all the food that is left, and hope they make it. Its like leaving your kids. I hope they stay with each other.

If you find them, please let me know. You can find me at V.A. Hosp.

Karcher, last four digits [of Social Security number] 9128.

P.S. Here is his eye med. Three times a day to clear up.

As Gary wrote the note, the ink in the pen was running out. He had to go over some letters several times for them to be seen. Barely legible, because of the lack of ink, was the information about the hospital. He had planned to include his neighbor's dog in the message, but the pen ran out of ink.

Gary found a plastic bottle with a screw-on lid. He folded up the note and stuffed it in the bottle along with the tube of eye salve. He found surgical tape and nylon string, and taped and tied the bottle to Himie's collar.

Then, early the next morning, Gary slipped out of the house without the dogs hearing him, because he didn't want them to follow. Fighting back tears, he walked away toward a staging area on Paris Road so he could be evacuated out of the area. "It's the hardest thing I've ever had to do," Gary said. "I cried like a baby. But I knew I had to leave them. The deputies said, 'No dogs.'" Gary was bused to an evacuee center at Camp Grover in Oklahoma. "When the computers weren't tied up," said Gary, who had never used a PC, "I had someone put up my name and information on the Internet, so my family would know where I was."

Meanwhile, on Tuesday, September 20, a Best Friends team was in St. Bernard Parish near the high school rescuing pets. I was with the team that day, near St. Bernard High School in Violet, when a driver in a pickup pulled up next to us. The truck had a cardboard sign taped to the doors that read "HSUS" (Humane

Society of the United States). The driver asked Mike McCleese, a volunteer from Cincinnati, and me, "Are you taking dogs? We found these two dogs together a few streets over. Can you take them?"

Inside the cab were two Dachshunds who'd been picked up near what we later learned was Gary Karcher's neighborhood. Mike said, "Sure," as I took one and he took the other. We handed over the Dachshunds to another team member, and the dogs were loaded into the air-conditioned transport van.

Two days later, three Best Friends team members were out rescuing animals in the same vicinity when they spotted a Rottweiler. Joe Huffman was walking on the residential street when he turned a corner. Sitting behind a bush, staring at him, was Himie. The other team members joined Joe to try to coax the frightened dog to them, but he would not budge. "We went through the routine, shaking the food bowl, talking sweet to him, but nothing was working," Joe said. Himie wouldn't leave his spot behind the shrubs. Then Joe poured water from a bottle onto the sidewalk. "When he heard that sound, he turned his head so fast I thought he was going to get whiplash." They were able to get a loop leash on him and then walked him to the van. Himie jumped right in and put his face in front of the air conditioner vent.

Himie's three rescuers—Joe, John Hoenemeier, and Chuck DeVito—noticed that the Rottie had something attached to his collar: the plastic bottle Gary had taped there.

That night, after the team returned to Camp Tylertown with a van full of pets, John pulled me aside and handed me the folded note, explaining that they'd taken it from Himie's collar. "Someone loved this dog. He took the time to write us," John said as he handed it over. Another volunteer pointed a flashlight at the letter, and, standing at the Ellis Island admissions area, I read it aloud. About a dozen volunteers—including several men— stood in a circle, their eyes welling up with tears, as they learned the saga of Gary and Himie.

The next day, I wrote a story about Himie and the message in a bottle and filed the article with my editor. That afternoon, it was posted on the Best Friends Web site. Within an hour, readers had located Gary at a refugee center at Camp Gruber, a military base near Muskogee, Oklahoma. Readers posted comments, letting Best Friends editors know that Gary had been found. One read, "I did a search and found this listing on MSNBC's log of messages from Katrina victims: 'Gary Karcher, 58, LA. Safe at Camp Gruber, Braggs OK.'" It was a combination of that Internet notice—the one Gary had someone write for him—and Gary's message in a bottle that led him back to Himie.

Within a few days, Gary was notified that Himie had been rescued and was staying at the Best Friends' temporary animal center in Mississippi. Because Gary's description of his mother's dogs did not completely match the two Dachshunds rescued two days before Himie, and three or four other doxies were at the center, photos of all the dogs were mailed to Gary in Oklahoma. He called Best Friends to positively identify the two small doxies handed over on the street by the HSUS as Precious and Pudgy, the "wiener dogs" he had described in his note. Rocky, Gary's neighbor's dog, was never located, however.

After Gary returned to Louisiana, he and his mother lived in a FEMA trailer on commercial property, where they were not allowed to have dogs. Himie continued living at Camp Tylertown until Gary could repair his damaged house. Precious and Pudgy were placed in foster homes a couple of weeks later. Before they were sent to their temporary homes, Precious gave birth to three puppies. She was isolated from the other dogs, but her puppies died three days later.

Meanwhile, a $5,000 insurance check covered the cost of a new roof and window repairs for the Karchers' house. Doing the majority of the work himself, Gary slowly began to restore his house, including electrical rewiring and hanging sheet rock, but the insurance money soon ran out.

Susie Duttge, who volunteered at Camp Tylertown and had met Himie, Precious, and Pudgy, learned of Gary's plight. From her home in Lake Forest, Illinois, she started a fund to cover the costs of building materials for Gary. She collected more than $4,000 so that Gary could make the house livable for him, his mother, and their dogs. Susie later helped two other families get their pets back home, too.

Nine months after Gary reluctantly left Himie and his mother's dogs, the Karchers were finally reunited with their pets. On May 16, 2006, the day Gary and his mother moved back into their home, Precious and Himie were driven from Mississippi for a reunion. Pudgy, who was still in foster care in Texas, was returned to them a month later.

Waiting in the front yard for Himie and Precious to arrive were Gary and Ethel. Gary grinned as Himie arrived at the Violet neighborhood in St. Bernard Parish. As soon as Himie got out of the car and stepped onto the sidewalk, his nose hit the ground and he ran all around the front yard sniffing. Then he greeted Gary by licking his hand. Gary dropped to his knees and hugged the dog he had written about. "Himie, you're home," Gary said. "Look around you, boy, you're home." Gary tossed a basketball in the front yard, and Himie fetched it and then dropped it at Gary's feet. It was just as it had always been. "I can hardly wait to get Himie in the boat again and take him fishing with me at the Delacroix marsh." However, he noted, after leaving Himie in the boat in the floodwater, "I hope he wants to get back in."

In July, when Pudgy was sent home to the Karchers, Gary was also given Himie's original collar, which still had remnants of tape on it. Presenting Gary with the original bottle was photographer Clay Myers. Instead of the note and eye salve, this time the bottle held cash. It had been passed around at a post-Katrina get-together at the Best Friends sanctuary in Utah, and employees had filled it with $400.

"I'll never forget this," Gary said. As for Himie, Pudgy, and Precious, Gary commented, "I know how lucky we are to get all three of our dogs back." He vowed to never lose them again. "There won't be a next time. I ain't leaving these dogs again."

For Ethel, seeing her son happy with their dogs safely home was what she had been waiting for since the storm. "All my stuff is gone," Ethel said, "but I have my son and our dogs. That's all I need."

Himie's saga is not only a story about how a dog weathered a hurricane after being left to fend for himself, but how his desperate owner, when ordered to leave his pet, searched for pen and paper so he could write a note, put it in a bottle, and tape it to Himie's collar. It is perhaps the most extreme example of how any identification on an animal can lead the pet home again. Gary made sure that if Himie survived, someone would know who he was.

Gary left not only his own dog behind, but also his mother's Dachshunds, Precious and Pudgy. He didn't know whether he would see them again, but at least he did something to make it possible.

Because of the letter, Himie, Pudgy, and Precious were returned to their original home. It is proof positive, those in rescue organizations say, that some sort of identification—whether an ID tag or microchip implants—is necessary to ensure that people's pets make it home in the event of a disaster.

Shanna Wilson also penned a letter, writing it as if it were from a cat. It did not get the cats home, but it was something she wanted the felines' new families to read so they would know what they had gone through.

Shanna had stumbled across a mama cat and her four kittens trapped in a waterlogged car and watched over them until she was able to humanely trap the mother. She took care of them while she tried to find somewhere for them to live. In late

October, she learned about Best Friends and drove the mother cat and kittens two hours to Camp Tylertown. Before she left New Orleans, she wrote the following letter so that their new care-givers would know their story.

My name is Calypso and these are my four surviving children after Hurricane Katrina. Thank you Best Friends! From the bottom of all five of our little kitty-cat hearts and from the bottom of the heart of the lady who rescued us all.

We were found on the floorboard of a flooded car on the west bank of New Orleans 10 days after the storm. Our eyes were not open and we were very weak from the storm. Miss Shanna Wilson, who works at the apts where the car was, heard our pitiful cries. Because our mom was afraid of people, Miss Shanna set a cat trap for her. It took 3 days to catch her but she checked on us 4–5 times a day. At times she would try to wrap us in cold wet towels to keep us alive because it was SO HOT IN THERE!

Once we were all together in this car, Miss Shanna fed momma three times a day to keep us healthy. She held us and loved us and for that WE LOVE PEOPLE. WE ARE FRISKY AND PLAYFUL and most importantly now FAT & HAPPY! Mommy has slowly come around. Although she is still a little skittish of people, love her tirelessly and soon she will rub up against you and paw at you to get your attention. Don't give up on her!!

Thank God for people like you. Pass our story around so we may be adopted by GOOD PEOPLE (only!!). If you can call Miss Shanna she would love to know where we all wind up!

Hurricane Katrina showed the world the intense relationship between humans and their pets. Some of the most compelling tales coming from the Gulf Coast following the storm were those about people forced, sometimes at gunpoint, to leave their animals behind. For many of those people, the only family they had left were their pets, according to New Orleans native Paul Berry, who at the time was chief operating officer for Best Friends Animal Society.

Dateline NBC's Rob Stafford, in a feature segment about Best Friends' rescue efforts, described people's pets as "the forgotten victims" of Katrina. He summed it up this way: "They were reluctantly left by their fleeing owners, left behind to live in a ghost town devoid of food, clean water, and most other life."

Many pet guardians put their own lives in jeopardy to stay behind with their animals; others were forced to say good-bye with little hope of ever seeing them again. Many *were* able, however, to get their animals back, or at least to hear that they had been rescued and were out of harm's way. The difficult lessons learned are many. The most basic message for pet owners, however, is that you need to attach some identification, such as an ID tag, to a collar with your name, address, and phone number. Even using a heavy-duty marking pen to print a phone number on a pet's fur as temporary identification works in an emergency.

7

Knock, Knock, Knocking on Heaven's Door

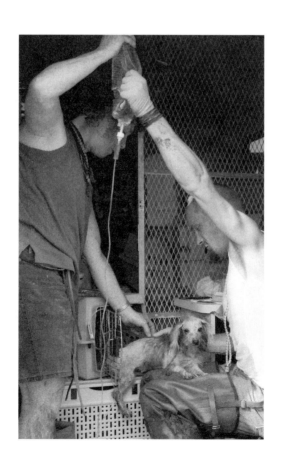

A DOG NAMED SCHMOO, reluctantly left behind like so many others, is perhaps the best example of the will to live that became engrained in the Katrina pets. Her love of people saved her life.

The six cats who stayed in their neighborhood, even though their owners did not know it at the time, are another inspiring example of the strong wills that kept these animals alive against all odds.

A dog referred to as the "Survivor" and later named Marina was able to make it on the streets for twenty-one days despite packs of larger dogs going after smaller ones. Marina tried to look invisible as she huddled between a chain-link fence and a potted plant, looking up at her rescuers with both fear and a hint of hope in her eyes.

These are their stories.

As Sergeant Cliff Deutsch carried a sick and fragile dog out of a storm-damaged house, it took everything he had to stop from slipping on the sludge as he descended the stairs. Schmoo, a female Boxer and Pit Bull mix, had been trapped inside the bathroom of her home for nearly thirty days without food or water.

Sergeant Deutsch, at the time a K-9 handler and officer with the Collier (Florida) Sheriff's Department, found the dog while conducting door-to-door searches. On foot that morning in a storm-devastated area in St. Bernard Parish, he heard a man call out from up the street that a dog might be upstairs in a nearby house. The words "1 dog rescued" were spray painted orange on the front wall of the house. On the walls or garage doors of homes, rescue patrols usually spray painted codes inside large black Xs indicating which homes had been searched, on what date, if bodies had been found, and if pets had been rescued or fed.

Cliff yelled back, "Are you sure?" and pointed to the front of the house where the writing was.

The guy hollered back, "Yeah. Go check it out."

Cliff prepared for the worst by gearing up with a pistol, department-issued fatigues, and a bullet-resistant vest—despite triple-digit temperatures. He was skeptical but decided to investigate anyway, hoping he would not come across the same scenario as the day before when the rescue team found two dogs crushed amongst the debris, as well as bodies of people. "You could tell the dogs had been trying to get out but couldn't," Cliff said. He also had come across another sad case. "We thought one dog was still alive," he said about a house he and others had searched, "but when we went in, the dog was actually curled up on the couch, dead, waiting for its master to come home." The next day, it still haunted him. But on this day, he held out hope as he walked into the house. He could not believe the condition, saying it was "was one of the worst I'd seen." Nevertheless, because the man on the street was so insistent, Cliff kept pushing his way through the debris. "I was slipping on the muck and the mud and tripping over everything," he said. "The house was destroyed."

Fearful that no animal could have survived long in a structure so damaged, Cliff remained optimistic as he searched the house. With another team member, he climbed over the rubble, pushed away debris and muck, and cleared a path to the top of the stairs. Once upstairs, Cliff stood still for a moment. That's when he heard a faint *tap, tap, tap*. He followed the noise to a closed bathroom door and forced it open. Inside a gunk-filled bathtub was a dog—skinny, dirty, and exhausted. Cliff didn't think she was alive, but then she started wagging her tail again. She was dehydrated, emaciated, and unable to bark. After all she had been through, she was able to muster up enough energy to wag her tail against the porcelain tub, letting her rescuers know she was there.

"Another guy and I pulled her out of the tub," Cliff said. "She was drained, and she could barely lift her head. It chokes me up thinking about it. She was skin and bones. Whatever energy she had was keeping her heart pumping. One more day, and she wouldn't have made it." As gently as he could, Cliff carried her down the stairs. *Don't drop her,* he told himself. *Don't slip, or she won't make it.*

He didn't wait until the end of the day for the van to return to the rescue center. Instead, Cliff took another vehicle from the caravan and rushed Schmoo back to Tylertown. He called ahead, and a veterinarian was waiting, ready to work on her. She was given fluids and immediate medical attention.

"I can still vividly see that scene of the rescuer carrying her to us," said Dr. Paul Levitas, a volunteer veterinarian at the center who ended up fostering the dog and taking her to his clinic in Cincinnati. The clinic staff named her Schmoo. "All I could see was a silhouette created by the dust and lights from the van of someone carrying a lifeless dog to me. It reminded me of that terrible picture of the fireman carrying the dead child in Oklahoma City. I still get emotional thinking about Schmoo that night."

Veterinary technician Kim Moore was also there when Cliff brought in Schmoo. "I thought she was dead, honestly, when I picked her up. The only thing that finally moved was her tail." After a day of fluids, volunteers lifted her onto her feet by using a towel as a sling. She weighed just sixteen pounds.

Also at the M*A*S*H Unit at base camp when Schmoo arrived was volunteer Catherine "Cat" Gabrel. "They put some fluids under the dog's skin, cleaned her up," Cat said. "She never struggled. She knew we were helping her. By the next morning, she started lifting her head. We called her Bathtub."

Three days after her rescue, Schmoo was driven to the Animal Hospital on Mount Lookout Square in Cincinnati, where she was slowly nursed back to health. "She was the worst we had seen," Kim said. "But every day she would get better and better." It took Schmoo a week and a half before she could stand on her own and another eight months before she was healthy and well socialized enough to be adopted. Schmoo's owners, who did not return to their home, have not been located.

Karen Wheat, one of the veterinary technicians at the hospital who helped care for Schmoo, adopted her months later. Today, she is "fat and happy," her caregiver says. Schmoo's favorite spot at home is on the sofa. "She's a very happy-go-lucky girl," Karen's friend Kim said about Schmoo, "and that tail is definitely always wagging."

Although volunteers like Cliff Deutsch made strong connections with the pets they rescued, people who'd lost their pets longed to reconnect with them. Such was the case with six cats from the Speyrer household, who survived without their owners for five months. It's another example of the bond household pets have with their humans. Even though no one was left in the neighborhood, the cats remained, waiting for their people to return.

When Betty and Gregory Speyrer returned to their East New Orleans home near City Park in late September, their six cats were nowhere to be found. For the next several months, Betty sent photos and notices to more than a hundred rescue groups across the United States. "I contacted them all," she said. "No one had them. I'd given up." After Hurricane Katrina, the couple had temporarily moved to Baton Rouge and were making arrangements to get a FEMA trailer set up on their property where they could live while their house was being renovated.

So, when six months after the hurricane Betty answered an early morning phone call, she could not believe what she was hearing. A worker told her that they'd gotten her "Lost" fliers and that Tiger, the Speyrers' tortoiseshell male cat, had been found near their house and taken to a temporary triage center. *It isn't true*, Betty thought to herself. *It has been too long.*

Betty hung up the phone, grabbed a cat carrier, and ran out of the apartment to make the seventy-five-mile drive to her storm-damaged home. If rescuers had found Tiger, the other cats could still be there, too, she thought. At the house, she got out of the car and stood there, listening. Then she called out, "Kitty, kitty." Nothing. Then, again, she called, "Kitty, kitty." Seemingly out of nowhere appeared Rainbow, their fifteen-year-old (and oldest cat), as if all he had been waiting for was someone to call out his name. Betty picked him up, held him for a moment, and then placed him in the carrier. She drove to Best Friends' temporary triage center, Celebration Station, in Metairie, just outside of New Orleans, to pick up Tiger.

After she arrived, she walked to his kennel, bent down, and looked inside. "Yes, it's him," she told his caregivers. "It's Tiger." Betty picked him up and held him against her. She pressed his face against her cheek, and they both closed their eyes. It was difficult to tell who was happier, Tiger or Betty. "Getting Tiger and Rainbow back the same day is incredible," Betty said. She gave a thumbs-up as she headed out the door with Tiger in tow, and then added, "Two down, four to go."

Indeed, about a week later Betty received another phone call from a rescuer telling her that yet another cat had been found near her home. This was Charlie, and he, too, was taken to Celebration Station. A week later Giuseppe was found. One by one, four of the Speyrers' six cats had been rescued.

The last two—Michael and Campenita—have been spotted in their neighborhood but have been too skittish to catch. Betty, now back on the property with her husband in a FEMA trailer, continues to leave food and water outside their home, hoping Michael and Campenita will return. Campenita, the shyest of their cats, was very attached to Michael, their black-and-white tuxedo cat, and Betty believes that is why Michael has not returned. "They played a lot and cuddled up all the time," she said. "Everywhere Michael went, Campenita followed. I think

Michael is staying out there with her." Michael has appeared a few times. "Michael's still not sure about coming in," Betty said, "but he's eating the food."

Meanwhile, the Speyrers' four other cats have settled back into the daily routines they had before Katrina. "The coolest cat is Rainbow, the yellow one," Betty said. "He's back to his old habits." One habit includes drinking water directly from the kitchen faucet. "He jumps on the sink, looks at us, and starts meowing for us to turn on the faucet. He's always done that, and we always turn it on for him and let it trickle down so he can sip from it. They all copy Rainbow's behaviors. They're back to their old ways."

And just as before, the cats are in and out between the house and the garden patio. "They like to go out in the garden at dawn and stretch and play around. We have grass again, and the garden is full of flowers. They enjoy it."

One new thing the cats have been doing since they returned home is sleeping in one of the upstairs bedrooms. The Speyrers for months afterward split their time between the FEMA trailer and the second floor of their home. One of the upstairs rooms was where they found Kelly, their fourteen-year-old dog, who didn't make it through the storm.

"Charlie sleeps under the bed, where Kelly was found," Betty said. "It's very sad. Kelly was like a mother to our cats. She groomed them and took care of them. When they were kittens, she would pick them up by the scruffs of their necks and put them in their basket. They miss her." When the repairs to their house are finished, the Speyrers plan to adopt a puppy for their cats. "Then the puppy can grow up with the cats," she said, "the way when they were kittens they grew up with Kelly."

Other pets left stranded survived, even though, unlike the Speyrers' cats, they were alone. When Clay Myers, a Best Friends staff photographer, spotted a lone Poodle darting across a yard in St. Bernard Parish on September 20, he nearly missed her because her hairless body was covered in soot the same color as the ground. He followed her to a yard, where she was about to jump into a large flowerpot, which was full of toxic sludge. "I wasn't going to let her jump in," Clay said. He bent down to grab her. She started to bite him. He pulled away and then tried to pick her up again. This time she let him. To him, it looked as if she was giving up. "Once I got her down from the pot, she was submissive," he said. "She had a look of shock and fear."

When Clay rescued the aging, balding, emaciated seven-pound Poodle that Tuesday, he was nearly overcome by the enormity of the event. One more life had been saved, and he was the one (with volunteer Mike McCleese from Cincinnati) who'd done it. "I looked into the eyes of the ones we rescued," he said, "and I know they were asking, 'Where did everybody go? Please get me out of here.'"

Marina, the Poodle, was one of the lucky ones. The rescue team knew that these dogs and cats had been without food or fresh water for more than twenty days. Deep down, no one expected to see a skinny toy Poodle survive the watery muck, which by then had dried into a two-inch-thick crust of gray toxic clay. Rescuers had not even been permitted to go into that section of town until a couple of days earlier. There was no way this dog would have survived one more day.

I was with the team that day, reporting on the rescues, when the Poodle was brought to the rescue van and started to crash. The temperature was about 105 degrees and it was humid. She closed her eyes, and her body started to go limp. Susan Thomas, a volunteer veterinary technician from Ashtabula, Ohio, watched as the dog was carried to the van. She ran up to us and asked, "Can I help? I have an IV bag in my van."

"Absolutely," she was told. "Do whatever you can to help her." Sue ran back to her van, grabbed the IV bag and a needle, climbed into the rescue van, and started giving the dog subcutaneous fluids. Sue and Josh, another vet tech from Ohio, whose last name wasn't known, continued hydrating the Poodle for an hour and a half. "We kept moving the needle in different places [across her back and shoulders]," Sue said, "making sure she got fluids everywhere, but we didn't know if it would save her." The dog began responding, and the life returned to her eyes. Sue searched the transport van for dog food. The only thing in a cupboard in the back were cans of wet cat food. "This should work," she said as she popped one open. She put some on her fingers, and the dog licked it from her hand. "This is why I'm here," said Sue, who had arrived a day earlier at Camp Tylertown with the Ashtabula Animal Protective League. "I have never, ever—and I've been doing this twenty, thirty years—seen a dog look like that: no hair, bony, the heat. We kept patting her down with cold packs, trying to get her temperature down." Helping save the Poodle, Sue said, "was probably the most rewarding experience I've had."

For the two-hour drive back to Camp Tylertown, we wrapped the dog in towels. On the way, the Poodle rested on my lap. We were in a pickup with volunteer Mike and photographer Clay, following the transport van back to base camp. The Poodle kept looking up at me, as if questioning where she was going. After a while, though, she settled down and fell asleep. When we arrived at camp, Mary Salter, a volunteer with Animal Ark in Minnesota, was standing near Ellis Island waiting to assist. I got out of Mike's truck, carrying the Poodle. "Can I help?" Mary asked. "Thank you," I told her. "She needs to see a vet right away." I explained that the dog had crashed after she was rescued, and that veterinary technicians had given her fluids to revive her.

Mary gently took the dog and ran with her the twenty or so yards to the M*A*S*H Unit, where a group of volunteer vet techs and a doctor were waiting for their latest animal patients.

The next day, Sue and Mary stopped by the triage center to see how the Poodle was doing. "Better," they were told. For Sue, it was a pleasant surprise. "I was bracing myself to learn that she hadn't made it," she said when she found out that the Poodle had survived. "She made me want to go out there and spend more days and stay longer. I was thinking, if she was out there, then there are more like her out there."

For the next couple of days, the Poodle mostly slept. Then Mary, who was touched by the little dog from the moment she met her, took her home to Minnesota and named her Marina.

Today, Marina is very much at home with Mary and two other canines. She has gained weight, her fur has grown back, and she looks like a Poodle again. An average day for her starts with a walk in the neighborhood. She's a playful dog, her new owner reports. "When we get back," Mary said, "she is usually so charged up that we play with her pile of toys until she is good and tired. She loves to play with toys—especially squeaky toys—but she'll play with anything she can find, like dirty socks." Then Marina often goes to work with Mary at the Animal Ark shelter. "I love to bring her to work with me so we can work on meeting new people and new dogs. She is still a bit fearful of new people and other dogs."

At home, though, Marina is queen of the household and rules over her canine housemates. "She makes it known that she is in charge," Mary said. "But she loves them and they love her." Every day, Mary said, Marina makes her laugh. "I am amazed every day that she has blossomed into a healthy, happy, fully furred little girl. It's truly a miracle. We don't know what we ever did before she was in our lives. I love her so much, and I am so thankful I took her into foster care. She is one special gal, and I can see to the depth of her soul through those precious eyes."

Marina struck Clay Myers the same way when she looked up at him on that hot afternoon as he rescued her. Afterward, he said he couldn't get the look in her eyes off his mind. Even though she was scared, he saw a flicker of hope in her eyes. It was as if she knew he was there to save her. "She's our poster child for Hurricane Katrina," Clay said. "She's a survivor."

8

It Takes Two to Make a Miracle

THE HEROIC EFFORTS OF INDIVIDUALS and their connection to the animals of Katrina helped the sick, the injured, and the frightened recover. Some volunteers had veterinary or nursing experience. Others were animal handlers or had experience at animal shelters or rescue organizations. It all added up to a wealth of knowledge and expertise for those dealing with the displaced pets at base camp, whose lives had been turned upside down. The animals expressed their gratitude in nonverbal and sometimes playful ways.

One example is Tenderfoot, a seven-month-old black Lab who was always happy, despite his footpads being burned off by the toxic sludge. National Guard officers had looked after him for a couple of days. Then rescuer Beth Montes happened upon their checkpoint, which also served as a military camp, and they handed Tenderfoot over to her.

It was during one of Beth's trips to the city to do house checks for pet owners that she stumbled upon Tenderfoot near the hard-hit Lakeview area of New Orleans, just below the worst levee break. "I was determined to get to two addresses," she said. "They'd each left multiple cats and dogs in their homes."

Beth drove her van into New Orleans from the west. "The city was deserted," she said. "I still don't know how I got in. I think I accidentally traveled down some side street from Metairie into New Orleans that wasn't guarded. There was only a small military presence in that area of the city, and one other civilian vehicle besides me was searching for animals. The officers were friendly, were glad we were looking for animals, and tried to describe the best routes into this still partially flooded area. I eventually hooked up with the Louisiana SPCA [Society for the Prevention of Cruelty to Animals] folks, and we took their SUV."

They drove to within about six blocks of the addresses. "It was clear nothing was left alive north of where we were," she said. "The devastation was total. Houses had been under water over their roof peaks. On the way out, after this disheartening experience, I retrieved my big van and was slip-sliding my way down the deserted streets."

That's when Beth came upon the National Guard checkpoint. "I think it was at Canal Boulevard in the Lakeview area where a uniformed young man with a gun waved me down," she said. "He asked me to drive over to their checkpoint, where he and his friends presented me with a black Lab pup."

They had found the dog wandering the streets several days before and had been sharing their MREs—or military-issued Meals Ready to Eat—with him. Each shift of officers handed him off to the next shift. "They kept him inside their vehicles," Beth said. "They were worried because the chemical burns on his feet and tummy were looking bad, and they didn't have access to vet care or any way to get him out of the city. They asked if I would take him. Of course, I did."

Beth put the pup on a back seat in her van, where "he immediately fell asleep. He was absolutely exhausted."

She made it out of the city and back to base camp with Tenderfoot. Soon, word spread around camp that a dog with no paw pads had arrived. Volunteers and staff embraced Tenderfoot and joined in to help bring him back to health. Volunteer holistic veterinarian and Buddhist nun Pema Mallu had set up temporary critical care in our office. This allowed each of us to take turns helping veterinary technician Nydia Alexander, also a Buddhist nun and a nurse in an Arizona hospital, take care of Tenderfoot while we ran in and out of the office doing our respective jobs. Nydia treated Tenderfoot and wrapped his paws in gauze. "All four pads were gone," she said. "He had burns on his belly, and all four feet were like raw hamburger. I used homeopathic calendula ointment, which is excellent for wounds like burns." Through it all, the pup never let out one whimper, even though his wounds were no doubt painful.

To keep him free from infection, the doctor ordered that Tenderfoot's feet not touch the ground. For bathroom breaks, Nydia carried him outside to a grassy area where no other dogs had walked. Then he was set down. Those of us in the office started taking turns with him. We had to be careful how we lifted him, making sure we didn't touch the wounds on the side of his body.

On the way in and out of the office, Tenderfoot relaxed and enjoyed the ride, wagging his tail the entire time. It was as if he knew that that's what he needed to do to get well again. When people in the yard approached, he'd wag his tail madly and lick their hands.

When Mike McCleese, a volunteer from Cincinnati, met the puppy, it was love at first sight and he applied to foster him. When he left base camp, he took Tenderfoot home to live with his two other Labs. Mike renamed him. "There's something about him that touches my heart. He's got a good soul, and he's laid back. That's why I call him Big Easy."

Mike's dogs, however, didn't take to their new housemate. Mike, who works at home and runs a landscape design business called A Guy and His Dog Landscaping, was disappointed. On a trip to his Vermont cabin—a second home for Mike and his dogs—he stopped near Erie, Pennsylvania, to visit fellow volunteer Mary Ellen Daub, whom he'd met at Camp Tylertown. She, too, had spent time with Tenderfoot. So, when Mike told her that his dogs weren't accepting Tenderfoot after more than a month, Mary Ellen jumped at the chance to adopt him.

Today, Tenderfoot lives with a handful of other dogs, has a dog door to run inside and outside at will, and is enjoying life. His wounds have healed completely, and he doesn't appear to have any side effects from his ordeal. Mary Ellen said he still has his puppy-like moments, typical behavior for young Labs. "He chews some," she said, "but he's a good boy. We're happy to have him."

For Scotty, a spiky-haired terrier mutt, it was two caregivers in particular who helped him overcome a severe case of heartworm disease so that he could go home to his original family a year later. Just after Christmas 2006, volunteer Darla Wolak drove Scotty to the house he'd hidden under just before the storm hit. "A few blocks from the house, he recognized the smell," Darla said. Once there, "he ran to his owner."

Bill Waiters and his family had been ordered to leave their home a day before the levees broke and the massive flooding started. They put Scotty in the back of their pickup and headed down the street. Scotty, who's quick and fiercely independent, jumped out of the truck and ran under their house. They turned around and went back for him, but Scotty thought they were playing chase with him, so he ran all around, in, and under the house. When the Waiters were ordered to leave again, they drove out of their neighborhood while Scotty stayed under the house.

Three months later, neighbors reported seeing a terrier running in the area. By that time, Best Friends and Animal Rescue New Orleans had set up the joint triage and feeding center at Celebration Station in Metairie. A feeding station where volunteers would leave bowls of food and water happened to be located across the street from Scotty's home. Darla believes that's how Scotty survived on the street.

Darla, who volunteered at Celebration Station, took the call about Scotty and responded by rescuing him from under the house. She wrote two notes and posted them on the house so that his family would know where he was. Then she took him to the center.

It was there that Laurel Ley, another volunteer, took Scotty under her care. He slept with her every night, and he played in the common area at Celebration Station when Laurel was downstairs working. "My heart fell for Scotty the first time I saw him in the medical unit at Celebration Station," Laurel said. She described him as "a loving, loyal, sweet dog. When we would go out, he'd carry his favorite toy with him—to go potty, to go outside, to go get food. The way he looked at you, your heart had to melt. Of course, Scotty perfected that look over time and used it ruthlessly."

He was the scruffiest, funniest terrier to entertain volunteers. Appearances, however, were deceiving. Scotty, who was grossly underweight, also had a bad case of heartworm; but a veterinarian recommended he not be treated until he put on weight.

So when Laurel headed home in mid-March 2006, Scotty went with her. But the fence around Laurel's home was too short for a tall terrier, so in April, Scotty went to live in Florida with Darla, who had two goals: to get Scotty past the heartworm treatment and to locate his people. "I found his owners, who had lost everything," Darla said. At that point, the Waiters weren't in a position to have Scotty live with them. She also learned from his family that Scotty's real name was Tweetie.

Next, three-year-old Tweetie began the medical regimen to eliminate the disease. "The summer was spent watching him breathe as he fought his way through heartworm treatment," Darla said. Tweetie survived and continued to gain weight. All the while, Darla stayed in touch with Bill Waiters and his family. By Christmas, the family was ready to take him, so Darla drove him home. She met the Waiters at their original home, where Bill was spending his days repairing the storm damage.

"As he ran to Bill and ran around the yard, I could tell Tweetie knew where he was," Darla said. "I drove away, and I looked at him sitting on the porch of the house, next to his owner, with his tail wagging, ears up, and happy. Tweetie was comfortable at the house and comfortable with the people. He knew it was his house, and he knew he was home."

Back at Camp Tylertown, workers in a cattery dubbed the Cat Barn quickly learned that a feisty feline named Petey was a challenge to care for. The orange tabby wanted nothing to do with them. He wouldn't let his caregivers touch him, and he tried to scratch them every chance he got. Just feeding him was a task. Still, workers dodged his claws and attended to his physical needs. According to caregiver Mckenzie Garcia, Petey wanted them to steer clear, so they accommodated him by giving him his space. It had been the same when he was rescued on October 6— more than a month after the storm. His family had left him upstairs when they evacuated, but at some point Petey had taken up residence under their house. To retrieve him, a rescue team had to crawl under the house and corner him.

When his caregivers witnessed Petey respond immediately to his family, who had learned that he was at Camp Tylertown, they were flabbergasted.

Once his family arrived, Petey became a different cat. Owner Sandy Ikenberry walked into the Cat Barn and called out, "Petey!" His back was to the door and he was curled up at the back of his kennel, but his response was immediate. He jumped up, swung around in his kennel, stared at Sandy, and then started meowing nonstop. "He's usually not a verbal cat," Lane Ikenberry said. But Petey wasn't used to living in a cage. At home, before Katrina, he had had free run of the Ikenberrys' home. Lane reached inside the kennel, picked up Petey, and held him against his chest. "I'm sorry we left you, Petey," Lane told him. "I'm so sorry." Petey fixed his eyes on Lane as if the cat couldn't believe it was really him.

"Wow. And we figured he might be an unlikely candidate for adoption because he was so grouchy," Mckenzie said as Lane cradled his cat.

"He's not grouchy anymore," Lane said. "He gets cranky sometimes at home, too. This ordeal may have changed his attitude." They left the Cat Barn with Petey safely inside a carrier for the ride back to New Orleans.

A Chihuahua-Dachshund mix named Ebony was hit by a car as three women watched in horror, too far away to prevent the accident. That dog, a small, frightened fear biter, would become my next foster dog.

I was volunteering in January 2006 when Ebony, limping and obviously in pain, arrived at Celebration Station from a hospital. From Ebony's paperwork, we learned more about her background, especially about how she'd been injured. Nancy Walsh, a refugee from New Orleans, had relocated to a busy street in Metairie and happened upon Ebony.

On December 18, 2005, Nancy and two friends were in a car when they spotted a tiny black dog darting across the busy street. When Ebony tried to cross traffic, a car hit her. The back tire rolled the small dog's body on the pavement.

Surprisingly, Ebony tried to get up to walk away but only succeeded in hobbling some. Nancy and her friends immediately ran into the street and picked her up before another car could hit her.

Ebony was stunned and in shock. Nancy described her as hurting and in bad shape. She wasn't wearing a collar, so they took her to a nearby veterinary hospital—the only one open in the area—where it was discovered that Ebony had a broken pelvic bone. On January 4, Ebony was taken to Celebration Station and put in a kennel. She wasn't happy being crated and cried a lot, so I began fostering Ebony, who later tested positive for moderate heartworm disease.

Near the end of the month, Ebony flew home with me to Las Vegas. A few weeks later, I drove her to the Best Friends clinic in southern Utah for her first heartworm treatment. At the time, she was the smallest dog the clinic had treated for heartworm, a disease that isn't common in Utah (although since then, the clinic has treated many more cases). A few days later, Ebony developed a 105-degree temperature, and I rushed her to a local emergency hospital, where she received a prednisone shot and was ordered to be on strict bed rest. Back home, I had to take Ebony's temperature twice a day to make sure she didn't develop another fever. I took her with my dogs on hikes or to the dog park, carrying her instead of letting her walk. She went along for the ride, her nose lifted to the wind and her ears flapping.

Even though Ebony had been through so much at the young age of two and a half, she adjusted well and showed her personality as an affectionate dog who loved to play and hike. Her pelvic bone healed on its own. Initially she was afraid of men and, for some reason, tall women, but after a few months, she adjusted to them. Nancy, when told that Ebony had survived, was pleasantly surprised because when she and her friends had dropped her off at the hospital that December day, they thought she wouldn't make it.

Seven months after I began fostering Ebony, Denise Jenkins, who lived in Utah, read a story about Ebony on the Best Friends Web site and applied to adopt her. Today, Ebony lives in Connecticut with Denise and her four other dogs, who each morning run together in a park bordered by woods. At night, she sleeps under the covers, guarding her side of the bed. Ebony, the smallest of her new canine family, rules the roost.

During the first week of January 2006, a team of trappers tracked a scruffy-looking feral-like dog they called Benji for seven days. They set a humane trap each day near where they'd spotted him, but he didn't fall for it. On the seventh day, they returned to check on the various traps they'd set, and when they got to one set for Benji—a six-foot-long trap in St. Bernard Parish—they found a calico cat inside. Alex Farr, one of the trappers, put on heavy protective gloves in case the cat decided to scratch him. After he picked her up, however, it was evident that she was a gentle—albeit frightened—cat. They didn't get Benji that day, but they did save a ten-month-old gray-and-white longhair cat, who was placed in a foster home five days later.

Dogs like Benji and cats like the gray, fluffy one were becoming more difficult to rescue. As the weeks turned into months, rescue teams depended on tips from residents, construction workers, and utility workers, who became their eyes and ears as to where cats and dogs were hiding in neighborhoods. Ads were placed in newspapers and public service announcements were given to radio and TV stations to alert residents to contact the rescuers if they saw any animals running loose. For Rex, an aging Chihuahua abandoned in a falling-down home, it was a neighbor who called in a tip to the Celebration Station triage center. Rex now lives in Jefferson, Louisiana, with Jeanette Althans, her teenage daughter, Emily, and their two cats. "He tries really hard not to chase them," Jeanette said. "But he can't resist." That's okay with Jeanette. "It's hard to imagine not having this happy little guy."

Life before Katrina was good for Rex. He lived in Uptown New Orleans. But after the storm, the house partially collapsed, and Rex's elderly person was moved to a rest home. Her family left the dog behind. Four weeks later, Best Friends volunteer rescuers Craig Hill and Anne Welling went to the house and found Rex under it. The house was partially caved in, which surprised them both, given that a senior citizen had continued living there after the hurricane.

Anne spoke with the neighbor who'd called the triage center to report that a dog was still there, but alone. She learned from the neighbor that the dog's name was Rex, he liked children, and he was about nine or ten years old.

It was by happenstance that Rex found his new home. In January 2006, Jeanette, who had been replenishing food stations for pets still out on the streets, stopped by Celebration Station to pick up more dog and cat food. Emily, twelve years old at the time, spotted Rex and asked if she could walk him. That was all it took.

"We weren't going there to adopt a dog," Jeanette said. "It was fate." Since going home with Jeanette and Emily, Rex has had medical issues, including abnormal blood-test results (now back to normal) and an eye problem (which has since cleared up). "My vet calls him the miracle dog," Jeanette said.

For now, Rex's health is good, and both Jeanette and her daughter cherish each moment with him. "I would adopt an older dog again," Jeanette said. "But I certainly hope we can enjoy Rex for a few more years. He is the perfect little dog."

In the case of a mother dog and her Dachshund–Cocker Spaniel-mix puppies, it took a team of volunteers nearly a day to retrieve them. Initially, one of the puppies, later named Puxley, led the team not only to her littermates but also to her mother. The canine family was safely retrieved from under a house after her patient rescuers held court for nearly twenty hours until the adult dog and pups were safely in their care.

It was late morning in early February 2006 when the tracking-and-trapping team received their daily assignment sheet at Celebration Station, which included a sighting of the lactating mother dog. She'd been spotted in an unpopulated neighborhood in Gentilly, in St. Bernard Parish. The team headed that way. When the group arrived, they noticed several houses with spray-painted letters on the front wall, indicating that people had been found dead inside. After much walking and searching, the group spotted a mama dog and her puppy on the street. The adult dog, frightened away by the rescue team, ran off, leaving her puppy alone. "We followed the puppy to see where she would go," said Barb Davis, who that day was with a team that included Rachel Laskowski, Kris Garvey, and Bill Daugaard. Puxley, the pup, walked to a nearby house and tried to climb the steps. "She was so little and the steps so big that her attempt was unsuccessful," Barb said. The pup then walked to the side of the house and hid in an opening under it. The rescuers followed her. That's when they heard the cries of other puppies. Two of the trappers shined a flashlight under the house and then crawled over debris as they followed the sound of puppies crying. They found the puppies tucked into a corner of rubble. They counted five, but the mother had not returned. "By this time, we were losing daylight," Barb said. Bill and Kris agreed to stay for however long it took the dog to return to her pups. It ended up taking all night. Bill and Kris sat quietly from a distance but still in sight of the makeshift home and waited for the mother to return.

At six o'clock in the morning—nineteen hours later—the mama dog went back to her pups. Bill and Kris quickly closed the opening to the basement and then called Rachel at Celebration Station; she, in turn, woke up Barb. They headed back to the neighborhood, crawled under the house, and plucked the puppies out. At one point, the team saw the papa dog—a black Cocker Spaniel—near the house too, but they weren't able to catch him. The mama and puppies were driven to Celebration Station to the puppy nursery.

After a five-day holding period, two volunteers, including Barb, each adopted one of the puppies. The other three went to New Orleans residents. The mother dog, who was later named Precious, was adopted, too. But a few days later, when the team returned to Celebration Station one evening after working in the field all day, they discovered that Precious had been returned by her adopters because she'd been having accidents in the house. That particular day had been a long one, so when Barb saw that Precious had been returned because she wasn't completely housetrained, Barb sat down with the dog, hugged her, and began to cry. "She's been living with her puppies under a house, where she gave birth, for five months," she said. "Of course she's not housetrained." Barb decided right then to take Precious home with her and Puxley.

On February 16, 2006, Barb, Puxley, and Precious flew out of New Orleans to Barb's home in Doniphan, Nebraska, to live with her husband, Lyle, and their Chesapeake Bay Retriever. Barb's adult daughter, Jennifer, later adopted Puxley—now named Madison. Precious and Puxley-Madison get together regularly to play.

A twenty-hour rescue of a mama dog and her pups may seem lengthy, but for an elusive dog named Bunker, the rescue took two months, as well as the perseverance of Best Friends rapid response team member Jeff Popowich and a determined gator hunter.

When Bunker, an American Staffordshire Terrier, was first spotted running loose in English Turn—a gated country-club community in the West Bank of New Orleans—he didn't want to leave. Who could blame him? The upscale homes there didn't sustain the devastating damage other communities experienced. During the flooding, it was a safe haven for Bunker. He knew a good thing when he saw it. Neighbors, however, weren't happy, mostly because of Bunker's looks.

Bunker, one said, fell into the pattern of potentially scary-looking Pit Bulls and related breeds who are often, in fact, spoiled house pets. Residents didn't recognize Bunker as one of their own. They were frightened, and so was Bunker, especially since a security guard and animal control officers had been chasing him for weeks. People who lived at English Turn watched each day as Bunker avoided officers by jumping into a man-made lake or by swimming across a moat to the other side of the golf course greens. Finally, a Best Friends rescue team was called to help round him up.

"There is a moat that goes between the houses and the golf course," Jeff said. "Bunker was living around the green on the ninth hole. He would swim back and forth across the moat, which was known to have alligators living in it from time to time."

But Bunker wasn't careless. "He is a smart dog who would keep his distance," Jeff pointed out. "I was able to find where he was sleeping and actually got close to him a few times. I would be able to get within a few feet of him, but I couldn't touch him."

The chase went on for several weeks until the homeowners association hired a gator catcher to trap Bunker. Jeff stayed in touch with the security officers and the trapper to make sure that when they caught Bunker, Jeff would be there to retrieve him. The trapper subdued Bunker using a tranquilizer gun while Bunker was on Lakeway Court next to the golf course. "He was able to catch him," Jeff said. "Bunker is a great dog, and I am just glad that he was caught and ended up with us."

Dogs like Bunker—Pit Bulls and related breeds who don't always get along with other dogs—can get into the wrong hands. So Bunker was transferred from Celebration Station to Camp Tylertown, where staffers called him Bunker Baby because of his affectionate disposition. Animal expert Sherry Woodard took care of Bunker. "When he's afraid, he tries to scare people," she explained. "It's all fear-based. When he's not afraid, he's the cutest thing. People fall in love with him when he's wiggly and playing with toys. He had to have been someone's spoiled pet at one time. That's the truth in shelter dogs across the country, because [the dogs] are so out of place." For Bunker, she noted, "It just takes time for dogs like him to change and make new friends."

In May 2006, when Camp Tylertown closed, Leah Purcell, an experienced dog handler who runs Spindletop Pit Bull Refuge in Houston, began fostering Bunker. Leah tried to find his family, but no one either working or living in the English Turn community knew where he had come from.

It took a long time, but in the summer of 2007, nearly two years after Hurricane Katrina, Leah Purcell found a home in Houston for Bunker as the only dog in a family. Bunker was a prime example of the follow-through that was done with so many of the Katrina refugee pets—all with the purpose of placing them in appropriate homes.

9

The Faces of the Volunteers

S ACRIFICING JOBS AND LIVELIHOODS and donating their time to save animals, volunteers placed their own lives on hold to rescue and care for other people's pets. Strangers, brought together by a disaster to save the animals because their owners were unable to, worked beside like-minded people and formed lifelong friendships. They were drawn to the Gulf Coast because of the images shown on TV of pets stranded on rooftops and debris floating in murky floodwaters. Compelled to help, people left their own pets and families and headed south.

Each day, new volunteers arrived at Camp Tylertown and, beginning in late December, at Celebration Station, all in the name of helping refugee animals. First thing in the morning, after the animals had arrived the night before, a handful of volunteers, along with a veterinary technician, took every new animal through the admissions process. They were photographed, microchipped, and vaccinated. Their medical paperwork was filled out, and any tag information from their collars was noted. Groomers kept busy decontaminating and bathing the newly arrived dogs, while caregivers washed and sanitized food dishes and then helped feed the animals. Then the animals were ready to be put in runs or kennels. Volunteers who didn't handle animals signed up for everything from cooking meals to typing data into the Petfinder Web site and a Best Friends database.

Everyone seemed to find his or her niche. Without fail, each new volunteer hit the ground running. When they arrived, many weren't sure exactly what their roles might be, but as soon as they set foot on the grounds of the hurricane relief center, they fell into step and pulled their weight. After one day, it was as if they had always been there.

Kelli Ohrtman arrived at base camp with Animal Ark, a Minnesota-based group, to write a freelance article for a local magazine. Instead, once at base camp, she had barely five minutes a day to write (although she did finish the article) because she spent most of her time helping care for and treat the dogs. "I worked in the triage area," said Kelli, who has veterinary technician experience and who eventually moved to Kanab, Utah, to work for Best Friends. "It was terrible. Our vet area was set up outside on a grass floor, and the love bugs were horrendous. Everything was covered in bugs. It was tough. Looking back, I can't even keep the months straight." She drove back and forth several times to Animal Ark's shelter, transporting animals the group fostered. The pull to return, however, was strong. "I think I was home for a week the first time, and I said, 'I have to go back.' It felt weird being home when I knew work needed to be done, and I knew how many animals needed help."

Christine Knierim, from Virginia, had planned to help with data-input records. Instead, when she arrived and saw the Pit Bulls in Pooch Alley, she devoted her time there. One dog in particular caught her eye. "I did not plan to bring a foster dog home when I went to Mississippi," she said. She had lost her Pit Bull, Arnold, a couple of months earlier and didn't want to try to replace him. "But after seeing all the kids who needed a place and knowing I had room for one, I couldn't help it. And the morning I saw Mr. Bo Jangles arrive at Pit Alley, I just felt in my heart he was the exact one who needed me."

Although many volunteers made new animal friends, Cathy Ramsey, a groomer, made new human friends—even one who lived near her but whom she hadn't met until they volunteered, coincidentally, at the same time. Cathy said the experience changed her focus from grooming to running a rescue center. She and her husband bought acreage and moved from Texas to California to start a small sanctuary. "Katrina was a tragic event," she said, "but out of that came people who opened their hearts for the animals."

While at the triage center in Metairie in January 2006, Cathy groomed Rhett Butler, a nine-year-old Beagle, for his TV appearance on ABC's *Extreme Makeover*, which filmed the reunion of Rhett and his family.

Working with the hurricane-affected pets was a life-changing experience for Sean Scherer, who was only twenty when he began his tour at Camp Tylertown in September 2005. He could not have predicted just how life-altering the experience would be.

Sean was scheduled to begin a two-year term overseas as a missionary for the Church of Jesus Christ of Latter-Day Saints at the end of 2005, something he was looking forward to and talked about for the nearly two months he was at camp. His work with the animals, however, had a profound effect on him, one that caused Sean to switch gears and return to college instead of going on the mission. In 2007, after completing his undergraduate work at Arizona State University, Sean went on to attend Southwest College of Naturopathic Medicine. He intends to become a naturopathic veterinarian. Hurricane Katrina, he said, changed his life.

After hearing about Katrina, Sean headed to Mississippi with his father, George Scherer, a Best Friends manager, to help wherever he could. By early November, just a month and a half before he was scheduled to leave for his mission, Sean made what he described as the most difficult decision of his life. He told his parents and his church, "I want to help animals. I don't think I was meant for the missionary." He didn't leave the church, just the missionary tour, which was a major decision because LDS men, as an expression of their faith, are expected to serve two years as missionaries.

Those of us working with Sean watched him mature into a gentle caregiver, and we observed frightened and shy dogs respond positively to his touch. Many referred to him as the "dog whisperer."

One night, Mickey Short, from Minnesota, was walking a dog at Ellis Island who'd just arrived from New Orleans. When the sound of a loud generator that operated the floodlights frightened the dog, Sean happened to be nearby. "I walked the first dog, and she started rolling like an alligator and spinning," Mickey said. "The trauma of whatever had occurred through the storm and its aftermath seemed to be in every muscle of her body." Then the dog stopped and looked back at Sean. "She hadn't known him any longer than she'd known me," Mickey said, "but she sure could read that there was safety within him."

Mickey told Sean, "She wants you." Sean sat down on the grass and told Mickey to sit down, too, so they'd be at the same level as the dog, and the dog relaxed. "Sean just has that way about him," Mickey said, "and dogs read it. That's why he is a whisperer."

In the following essay, Sean describes his time at camp:

We are all truly human, and it is embodied in our souls to fall in love. In my case, it was with a dog. I was working with new arrivals one day and a huge Rottweiler named Chopper came in. He was way too sick for us to do anything with him, but I saw a special spirit in his eyes, so I took him to the veterinarian. The vet said he was extremely dehydrated. We put him on fluids right away.

After starting the fluids, the doctor found an enormous soft lump on the side of his rump and started examining him. She found that the lump was filled with a greenish brown puss and she couldn't figure out what it was. So, we sent the blood work off to a clinic and waited for the results.

Every night and day I would go in and sit with Chopper, to be with him. He couldn't even move, he was so weak. I would go in his kennel and lift his head into my lap to massage his face. I could see it in his eyes that he loved what I was doing and appreciated it. Without moving or making a sound he emitted an aura of love. After two days of this, I passed by his cage and he popped his head up to bark at me and get my attention. He did it to spend another bit of time [with me].

The next time I talked to the vet she told me hesitantly that he was dying, that he had cancer and heartworm [disease] and would probably be dead soon. Hearing that hit me so hard, I lost my breath for a moment and felt that sincere love and desire not to lose him, not to lose that spirit that was embodied within that immobile body.

It was hard to come to the realization that he might be gone soon, but I decided that he wasn't going to die without getting the most out of life. I was going to love him regardless. I thought about the attachments that we make with living things and the way they seem to dissipate when you lose the physical being you love. I realized that the only truly noble thing to do in this kind of situation was to love regardless of what the future may bring, because that is truly when love should exist, right now.

As time went by with Chopper it seemed he wasn't making any sort of turnaround, until one beautiful day when I walked by and saw him standing up in his crate asking for a walk. So I took him out, and walk he did.

Limping but determined, he strutted as though nothing had happened, as though he were truly a dog. Over the next few days, he kept getting a little tougher and more determined. He was getting better! Then I asked the vet about him again and she said, "It's amazing. Chopper is going to be all right." So I got to witness the miracle of survival and love intertwined to create an amazing bond between two different species. I had the honor of placing Chopper out into the general population here. It was an uplifting joy to proudly walk him to his new home.

Being here has been an all-around uplifting experience. I have met incredible people and have experienced incredible things. I have seen the spirit of many dogs completely turn around. I work with the intake crew here during the day. I handle all of the dogs that come through, so if somebody should be bitten it should be me, but these scared dogs do not want to bite, and I haven't been bitten during the processing yet. Some dogs come in very scared and stupefied with their new situation. They wait in the corners of the runs, waiting for someone to approach them. Often they growl and sometimes they snap, just like you would expect of such a displaced creature. I have found that gently wrapping their heads with a blanket and holding them closely to your body for a long time creates a new safety net that the dogs rely on. They start hugging your body. I release the blanket from their heads and the once snapping, so-called aggressive dog is calmed and comfortable with his or her new life. This is one of the most amazing things that I have ever experienced. I feel like such a part of the whole nurturing process for these animals.

At night my duties change. I become a computer guy, working with all of the database information and pictures of the animals. Most importantly, I get the opportunity to work with some of the most amazing people that I have ever met. Here at the Best Friends rescue center, you get the honor of seeing the essence of human kindness that is often overlooked in our society.

Sean was one of many volunteers, along with Mickey, who each day watched the dogs and cats arriving at Ellis Island, lost and frightened, and then witnessed them come back to life as the pets began to realize that the worst was over. It was a sight to see. The animals recognized that they were finally out of the storm, out of harm's way, and in safe hands once more.

Witnessing that daily transformation drove the volunteers.

At the end of each day, around six thirty, the cook assigned that evening would call out on the bullhorn that dinner was ready. According to Best Friends founder and animal consultant Faith Maloney, dinner at Camp Tylertown was "a time to gather and talk about the day. New volunteers are arriving every day, so this is often their first chance to size up their coworkers and get the feel of the place. Advice is handed out, like how to avoid stepping in a nest of fire ants or how many sweaters to wear in the mornings before the sun comes up."

The conversation at the picnic tables often turned to "Where are you from, what do you do there, and why are you here?" Faith pointed out that during her three days at base camp, she met "people from all walks of life, all ages and skills, and all parts of the country." One was Beth, an executive whose last name wasn't known, who was on company time as a way of promoting volunteerism among its employees. "I saw her earlier in the day clearing out a messy shelf area and sorting out supplies," Faith said in November 2005. "She headed up the team that cooked dinner that night and was about to recruit clean-up volunteers from the newbies." Camp Tylertown, Faith said, "has had a profound effect on so many people. Animal lovers are special people, and this has given so many of us a chance to help animals who need that help so desperately. I'm seeing some lifelong friendships in the making."

Also helping the animals in a big way was Nydia Alexandra, a nurse and Buddhist nun, who said that caring for the pets of Katrina was monumental in her life. "It definitely was a life-altering experience," Nydia said, "just to be in the midst of intense situations, but then have these animals, the smallest things, so grateful. If we had to do treatment, almost all of them just looked up at us and simply let us do it. It filled my heart."

At times, though, the work was overwhelming. "Sometimes," Nydia said, "I had to have a good cry just because it was so intense and there was no escaping or running away from it, because they needed our help. We started early and worked late. I will never forget it. It really was extraordinary."

So extraordinary, she said, that "it's something that changed all of us and does bind us all, the depth and the breadth of the experience. It was huge." Afterward, "when I came back to work at the hospital, I was sort of shell-shocked."

Still, Nydia wouldn't change a thing. "I would do it again. I was really grateful to have had the opportunity to go. I'm sure when the next disaster hits, we'll go and do whatever we can do. It's so bonding because you have this little window of time and space to make a difference for as many as you can."

A lung illness didn't deter volunteer veterinary technician Chandra Signmund, who first worked with Alley Cat Allies and later Best Friends at Celebration Station, running the cat triage with Mike Bzdewka. She traveled to New Orleans for three tours. Chandra adopted a cat named Noni after the owner told her he could no longer properly care for the cat. As the owner handed the cat to her on a New Orleans street, Chandra promised that she'd find her a good home. Chandra kept her word. At the end of February, she took the cat with her to Long Beach, California, to live with her and her husband's other two cats. After she returned home, Chandra discovered that her lung problem appeared to have been caused by the particles in the air following Hurricane Katrina.

For Jan Martin, a veterinary technician, volunteering meant jumping around from area to area at Camp Tylertown to do whatever was needed. She volunteered in October, went home, and returned for two more stints. She made friends with people she's still in contact with. "The way I describe it," Jan said, "is that we were a group of people who, had we not met in that particular event, probably wouldn't socialize with each other. But we were thrown together, and we all had a common goal."

Jan took home a kitten named Ziggy. All the pets rescued and taken to either Camp Tylertown or the Celebration Station triage center had their photos and information listed on the Internet. So, once home, Jan regularly checked lost-and-found sites, hoping to find Ziggy's person. No one came forward. "He came in one night with two other kittens," she said. "He was rescued from an elementary school in St. Bernard Parish. The next day, I did his blood work. He was a mess. He was covered with muddy water, and he didn't make a sound. He is just the sweetest little kitten. Then he got really sick with the upper respiratory infection."

Now at home with Jan and her family, Ziggy, who has recovered, is "more than just a reminder of Katrina. He's just one of

the most amazing cats I've ever known. We bonded so strongly."
As a vet tech, Jan had worked at base camp with both dogs and
cats. Sometimes, especially when the pets arrived in bad shape, it
was difficult. She didn't return to her job as a vet tech at a for-
profit animal clinic. "I didn't want to go back and work in a hospital immediately," she said. "I felt like it was so money-driven."
Jan no longer felt at home in a hospital environment. "I got more
gratification from helping for no pay," she said.

The pull to continue helping was so strong for one volunteer that
he extended his stay at camp by seven months. Chuck De Vito, an
engineer from Minneapolis, had planned to stay less than a
month when he took a three-week leave of absence from work.
Instead, he quit his quality-assurance job with a biotechnology
company to remain in the Gulf region until May 2006. He arrived
at base camp in a minivan on September 17, nineteen days after
the storm. When he made the decision to stay longer, he called
his boss to say he wouldn't be returning. He also left the farm
he'd shared with two other people where he had helped care for
a mule, three miniature donkeys, rabbits, goats, chickens, and a
pot-bellied pig.

"I was originally set up to come here with the Red Cross, and
I saw a link to Best Friends on CNN's Web site," Chuck explained.
"I said, 'You know what? I'm going there.'" And he did.

For the first few months he lived in his van, which he'd
equipped with a nylon lean-to and a bunk he'd built. When the
weather started to cool, he ordered a large tent. By then, he was
caring for an aging Chihuahua whose owner was never found.
Chuck named him Bang Bang. "We found him under a car in
New Orleans on September 29," Chuck said. "He's content and
happy, and he's glad to be with me. He is old and missing his
front teeth. I think he's homely looking, but I adore him."

Chuck helped rescue some of the toughest and highest-
profile cases, including Himie, the Rottweiler found with a

message in a bottle taped to his collar. Another of Chuck's cases was a dog called Boyfriend, so named because animal expert Sherry Woodard was the only one the dog would allow near him; everybody called the dog "Sherry's Boyfriend." And there was Tripod, a three-legged Staffordshire Terrier who chewed off her own leg to free herself from the mechanism inside a sofa bed. Tripod was a favorite of the volunteer caregivers. "Tripod was one of the ones I adored," said Catherine "Cat" Gabrel. "There were only one or two Pit Bulls we couldn't handle. But Tripod just warmed your heart. You just wanted to pull her up on your lap and hold her. Tripod was always easy to handle."

She wasn't so easy to handle during her rescue, however. "It took four of us two hours to get Tripod and Boyfriend," Chuck explained. "We had to barricade them using a kitchen table and a refrigerator to keep them confined so we could get them."

Because he was involved in animal rescue in New Orleans, "That experience really imprinted on me, and I decided I couldn't go back to that other life for a while." After a few weeks, Chuck took on other jobs, including power-washing endless numbers of plastic transportation crates. "Crate washing is like a never-ending pile of dirty dishes, but I pretty much do whatever anyone asks of me." Then there was trash detail, which he worked with Best Friends' former human resources manager, George Scherer. "If the head of human resources can do trash detail in the morning, then I can do the trash detail, too," Chuck said.

Still, to him, the experience was extraordinary, especially with the new friends he made. "I haven't experienced this type of thing since I was in the military," he said. "It's the kind of closeness people have that you don't usually experience in the real world."

It was the same for Don Arnold, a Vietnam veteran who had not left his home state of Maine since his release from the United States Marine Corps in 1975—that is, until Hurricane Katrina struck. He was watching news about the hurricane in early September 2005 when his phone rang. It was his friend Ronnie Lott, a veterinarian who had retired to Florida. "He called and asked if I was crazy enough to go down to New Orleans with him to rescue animals so he could treat them." They planned to be gone two weeks. "I stayed eight months."

In the service, Don said, "Marines are like your brothers. You live with them and spend twenty-four hours a day with them." That's how it was for him in New Orleans. The real heroes of Katrina, he said, were "the volunteers, from fifty different states. They weren't being paid. They did it on their own. That impressed me. The people who were cleaning the crates, rehabilitating the animals, taking care of them after we rescued them, they're the heroes. Every single person who went down there made a difference. These people to me now are more like family than friends."

Don shut down his contracting business, a career he'd worked at for thirty years, to remain in New Orleans. "The animals were what the whole thing was about," he said. "The one rescue I'll always remember is a Pit Bull mix who came running down a corridor in a house, straight toward me. I thought he was going to attack me. But he ran as fast as he could, right past me, out the door, down the porch stairs . . . and jumped right into the Big Nasty [a Best Friends rescue vehicle]. He turned around in the van and looked at me like he was saying, 'Let's go.' It made me laugh. He knew exactly why I was there. That was the easiest rescue I did. I'll always remember it." He's worked on a few rescue efforts since. Doing anything else, for him, is no longer an option: "I'll do this the rest of my life. I'll never go back to contracting. I'm hooked on animals. How can we not help them? They're helpless without us."

Barb Davis, a volunteer from Nebraska, worked with Don in the field. One day, in the Lower Ninth Ward, Barb told Don that she wanted to show him something she'd seen the day before. They walked to the spot. "Look at this," she told him, pointing to a large pawprint. "That's from a German Shepherd," he told her. The dog was nowhere in sight. Early the next morning, however, Don returned to the Lower Ninth, this time with roast beef in hand. He sat down and waited. A while later, he spotted the dog, who did turn out to be a German Shepherd. "He growled at me,"

Don said. "I tried to get him to come to me, but he kept growling. I got close enough, slipped a cloth loop-lead around his neck, and he came with me. That dog's foot was bigger than my hand, but he only weighed fifty pounds. I named him Chance." By the time Barb woke up that morning, Don was already back at the triage center with Chance. It was Don's turn to show something to Barb. He walked her to the kennel where Chance was housed. He told her, "I got the German Shepherd." Chance soon left the center for a German Shepherd rescue group to recover.

Days like those in the field with fellow rescuers, Barb said, "were pretty special. Don and I will be friends for life."

For Carol Guzy, a Pulitzer Prize–winning photojournalist, staying in the region meant taking a leave of absence from her job as a staff photographer at the *Washington Post*. She had gone to the area with a reporter a week after the storm to cover the plight of the human refugees for the *Post* and was scheduled to return home after about a week. The pull of Katrina, however, caught her after she witnessed stranded animals. Instead of leaving, she remained in New Orleans for several months, but this time she was on her own. She hooked up with several groups, including the crews on U.S. Fish and Wildlife Service boats, who were assessing—but not rescuing—the animals. Like almost everyone down there, she operated on very little sleep. She went to Camp Tylertown a couple of times and, later, to the Celebration Station animal rescue center, from December until the end of February 2006, when it closed its doors.

Cherie Fox and her husband quit their jobs in Ohio and moved to Mississippi so Cherie could work for the St. Francis Animal Sanctuary. She stayed there a year, "got it out of her system," as she put it, and returned home to work on plans for starting her own sanctuary.

After spending time in Tylertown and rescuing animals on the streets of New Orleans, John Hoenemeier, who worked in the computer industry in Los Angeles, decided he no longer wanted to "push a pencil." Katrina showed him that. He moved to Kanab, Utah, to work for Best Friends and then trained in his spare time to become an emergency medical technician (EMT). Today, he works in Kane County, Utah, as an EMT.

I, too, am included in that group of people who made split-second decisions about whether to stay at or leave Camp Tylertown. When Katrina hit, the semester had just started at the University of Nevada, Las Vegas, where I'd been teaching four classes each semester for five years as an adjunct journalism instructor. When I was asked to travel to the Gulf Coast, I enlisted substitutes for my classes and headed south for what I'd expected to be two and a half weeks. But at the end of that time, Best Friends asked me to stay on. Back then, I had no idea they would later offer me a full-time writing position. Still, without hesitation, I agreed to stay. I understood exactly why Chuck De Vito and John Hoenemeier didn't want to return to their jobs, to what Chuck called "the real world." The animal rescue effort wasn't over. Pets were still in harm's way, and the desire to stay and help them was a powerful magnet.

Not everyone quit their jobs or relocated to other cities or states after helping the pets. Yet the experience for many was life-changing nonetheless. Cat Gabrel said that working with the displaced pets gave her a new outlook on life. "It changed the way I think about things and perceive the world," she said.

She traveled to Camp Tylertown in mid-September with her brother, Gary Gabrel, and his girlfriend. "Getting to go and help animals was the right fit for me," she said. "It was so amazing. You had thousands of people showing up to help animals. They didn't care what kind of animals they were. Everyone did everything they could, twenty-four hours a day. Nobody complained. It was life-changing.

"If I regret anything," Cat explained, "it's that I didn't work enough. It's the best experience, besides childbirth, I've had."

10

Red Gets His Wheels

FOR THE MANY VOLUNTEERS who cared for a young, partially paralyzed dog named Red during his lengthy journey from the storm to finding a home, the disabled Staffordshire Terrier represented more than just a rescued Katrina victim. To them, Red was a mascot, the poster boy for Katrina pets. Volunteers embraced the handsome, red-nosed dog, and he returned the affection with vigor.

After he was left homeless by Hurricane Katrina on August 29, 2005, Red hung out behind a New Orleans house where a resident going in and out of the area began leaving him food and water. But on November 5, Red was struck by a truck maneuvering the rubble-strewn street, leaving the dog paralyzed from his middle torso down.

Many pets rendered paralyzed by a car accident are put down. When Red was first examined in early November at an emergency hospital, the vet and technicians hoped that it wouldn't end in euthanization for this dog. When they realized Red had a huge will to live, that potential outcome was pushed aside.

Red's journey from the brink began on that cool November night. Bloody trail marks across pipes and debris on the road and driveway indicated that Red had dragged himself, possibly injuring himself further, back to the house where he'd been hanging out. He curled up behind a broken-down air-conditioning unit in the backyard. The owner of the house discovered the injured dog and phoned the Best Friends triage center at Celebration Station in Metairie, telling them it was an emergency. Two rescuers—Best Friends' Jeff Popowich and volunteer David Halperin—were dispatched to the house.

The two men rescued Red from his hiding place in the backyard. Conscious but in bad shape, Red simply lay there, looking up at them. Skin was missing from his shoulders and face, and he had lacerations all over his body. Worse, he did not appear able to move his back legs.

David and Jeff lifted Red into a carrier and then rushed him to the Southeast Veterinary Specialists in Metairie, where Red would stay until early January. The hospital was serving as an emergency facility for Katrina pets. Red had fractures of the third vertebra and tenth rib. Besides the fractures, he had scrapes, cuts, and lacerations on his body, legs, and head. "He was beat up and in shock," surgery technician Alice Louviere said. "He had the shakes, but he licked us. As I put his IV catheter in, the whole time he licked my hand. Never one time did we consider putting Red down, just because of his spirit." That Saturday night, Red had surgery; rods and a plate were attached to put his fractured vertebra back together and hold it in place. Best Friends paid for that, plus, according to Alice, a second procedure that was done to remove a rod that had shifted.

Other dogs and cats also went to that hospital, which before the storm had been a veterinary clinic. After Katrina, it became an emergency hospital that continues to operate today. "We had tons of cats from Best Friends who weren't eating," Alice said. "At one time, we had thirty cats with feeding tubes, and they were all given a chance. God only knows what they'd been through. We had some for whom it would take a week to act like a dog or cat again."

Like Red, a cat named William Tell was given a second chance, one he lost two weeks later. His story was broadcast across the Internet. William Tell was rescued on January 3, 2006, by a team from Celebration Station who found him with an arrow in his chest. The arrow had gone through one side of his abdomen and exited through his chest. When William Tell arrived at the hospital, he was able to sit up, even though the arrow stuck out from either side. After surgery, he continued to do well and the prognosis looked good, but then he took a turn for the worse. "He started eating on January 7," Alice said. Then, on January 15, he went into cardiorespiratory arrest. "We attempted to resuscitate him several times," Alice said, "but we never got him back."

For Red, the outcome was the opposite. In the same hospital where the staff had tried so hard to save William Tell, Red spent the next two and a half months rehabilitating. A team that included veterinarians, vet techs, and surgery technician Alice took care of him. The veterinarian who performed the surgery was Dr. Rose Lemarie, a board-certified surgeon who owns the hospital with her husband.

"We all had a very strong bond with Red, and there was not a dry eye when he left," Alice said. "He was loved by all of us. When he left, we knew he was going to be taken care of, but he was here with us for three months. I spent many days and nights lying on the floor with him in our treatment room. He could always bring a smile to my face."

The hospital was the only one open in the area at the time. Its doors were kept open for rescue groups twenty-four hours a day during those first few months. "Animals such as Red," Alice noted, "make us who we are."

Red's caregivers manually moved his legs as part of his rehabilitation. They also used water therapy. The hospital has a heated indoor pool for rehab, and Red was able to go in the water after he had healed enough. Three times a week, a hydrotherapist worked with him in that pool. "He swam his behind off," Alice said.

David visited Red once a week at the hospital, and Red was always eager to play. For David, who stayed in the region for a few months to rescue pets, Red was the highlight of his trip. If he had done nothing else, he said, rescuing Red alone would have made the effort worthwhile.

On January 9, 2006, Red was transferred to the Celebration Station triage center and had just a one-day return visit to the hospital in February for a bad case of mange. As soon as Red arrived at the triage center, volunteers doted on him, and some even put their sleeping bags in his playpen to spend the night with him. A laminated kennel card was attached to his pen (which was about ten by eight feet and just three feet high, making it easy for volunteers to step in and out to visit him). The card was an open invitation to volunteers.

Hi! My name is Red. I am about a year and a half old and love attention. I was hit by a car in November 2005. They operated on my back, but I am still paralyzed in the hind end. I can't control my bladder, so if I pee will you please help clean up.

I like toys to chew on and people to pet me. Feel free to come and visit me!

On January 11, for the first time, Red was let out of his playpen—a corner of the room at the former arcade—and allowed to scoot on his rump around the room. It happened on an evening when volunteers Tasha Corrigan and Fiona Archer of Toronto said their good-byes to fellow workers by throwing an after-dinner party. It was the last night of their five-day tour. They served up cheese, crackers, dip, and grapes to celebrate their time helping the animals. Diane Smith from Texas put a bouquet of flowers in the center of the mess table. Then a handful of people played a form of the television show *Fear Factor* to see who could eat the most fruit and vegetables.

The highlight of the get-together, however, was when Red was allowed to scoot around on the floor and play with people and some of the staff's foster dogs. For the first time since being released from the hospital, Red was mobile. Red's face when he realized he was moving on his own steam and mingling with volunteers was a sight to see. One after the other, volunteers called Red to them. He slid up to one, then moved on to another. His face lit up as he scurried and scooted as fast as he could. Clearly, Red did not know he was disabled.

The next morning, the world was introduced to the handsome, partially paralyzed dog after Best Friends posted on its Web site a story I wrote about Red that included a photo (taken by volunteer Barb Davis) of him playing with a toy. Several animal welfare sites picked up the story, marking the beginning of Red's notoriety. New volunteers would walk into the triage center and ask, "Where's Red?"

It was clear Red needed to be more mobile so that he could go outside for exercise and fresh air. But he couldn't scoot around on his rump outside on the pavement because he might hurt himself. A request went out and, at the Best Friends sanctuary in Utah, a couple of staffers went to work searching through donated items until they found an aluminum wheelchairlike cart for dogs. It looked like it would fit Red. The cart was immediately shipped to Celebration Station, and a couple of volunteers adjusted it to fit Red. When he got in the cart for the first time, the look on his face was almost one of surprise. It was as if he couldn't believe it. He ran around in circles on the carpeted floor.

Outside, on the blacktop road circling most of the Celebration Station building, Red ran like the wind. As if by instinct, he cornered and backed up in the large parking lot like he was Mario Andretti. As word spread at the triage center that Red had wheels, volunteers gathered outside, some with their hands over their mouths in amazement. Many had tears in their eyes. It was a pivotal moment in Red's life. In the blink of an eye, he went from being an immobilized dog to running around on a road with people trying to keep up with him. He had a profound look of concentration on his face. Red was free. And he knew it.

Everyone going in and out of Celebration Station knew about Red. They couldn't miss him. When Red wanted attention, he would first bark quietly. If no one responded, it escalated to a howl. Volunteers would run to Red: "Poor boy," they'd say to him. "What do you need, Red?" They'd step into his playpen and spend time with him. Best Friends staffer Mike Bzdewka, who ran the cat section at the center, often moved his sleeping bag to Red's playpen and spent the night with him. Red soon figured out that howling, whimpering, and barking were his tickets to companionship.

Red became even more famous when he led the Best Friends contingent at the February 2006 Barkus Parade through the French Quarter. When Red passed by the podium in his cart, a resounding cheer was heard. He wore a T-shirt, a dog jacket, and Mardi Gras beads, and looked proud as he marched through the streets. His debut at the parade was broadcast on the Internet via streaming video.

Red was fostered out to Spindletop Pit Bull Refuge in Houston by its founder, Leah Purcell. Leah began dropping Red off for day care at the Longwood Animal Hospital and Pet Resort, a rehabilitation center for animals in Cypress. There, after weeks of therapy, Red got some feeling back and started wagging his tail for the first time. He also began sitting up for treats, bracing his weakest leg against a wall. Although he will always be paralyzed, these strides have helped him better maneuver when he's not in his cart.

A CNN news crew shot video of Red at Celebration Station, just before his transfer to Houston, and a broadcast of the video led to a permanent home for Red. The crew accompanying newsman Anderson Cooper stopped by the center and filmed Red scooting around inside, his feet and legs wrapped in gauze to prevent rug burns. A few days later, the piece aired on CNN's *Anderson Cooper 360* show. That's how Diane McDermott from Boynton Beach, Florida, first learned about this special dog.

Leah and Diane were put in contact with each other, and Diane applied to adopt Red. Leah enlisted a friend who lived nearby in Florida to do a home visit, to see what Red's home environment would be like. Diane removed her bed's box spring and put her mattress, which she covered in a plastic sheet, on her bedroom floor so Red could get onto it easily. She lined a kiddy pool with crib padding and filled it with toys. Then, on May 29, Diane drove two days and eleven hundred miles to Texas to pick up Red.

Red couldn't leave the Longwood day care without a big send-off, given that he had stayed there for nearly three months. While there, Red was doted on. During the day, he was moved from his kennel to veterinarian Lucy Gillespie's office. Some nights and weekends, she even took Red home with her. During the week, employees regularly took him outside to play ball in his cart.

It was a bittersweet good-bye. "Everybody is very attached to him," Lucy said. "We all were crying. I'm going to miss him, but I'm also happy he's going to have a one-on-one relationship with someone who has time to work with him. Diane is going to do great. That's the whole point of fostering," Lucy continued, "to prepare them for going into permanent homes."

The day before Red left, a veterinary technician provided doggie ice cream, and everybody gathered around Red for the farewell party. Then, on the day he left, employees showered him with going-away toys, tennis balls, and his favorite chewies. For the trip home, his new mom, Diane, bought him a black-and-orange Harley-Davidson T-shirt and a seat-belt harness. His belly belt (to hold up a partial diaper) was put on, and he was strapped into the front seat of Diane's rental car. A Houston TV news crew was there to record Red's big send-off.

"He was sitting in the front seat of Diane's car, ready for the ride," Lucy said. "He thought all the attention was the coolest thing ever. He didn't look back."

The next evening, Anderson Cooper did a follow-up piece and informed CNN viewers of Red's adoption. Video was shown of Red running at high speed in his cart around the perimeter of Longwood's dog park. Anderson described Red as an amazing, happy dog and wished Diane and Red well.

Since arriving home in Florida with Red on June 1, 2006, Diane has continued his therapy by massaging and keeping his back legs moving and manually exercised. Although he's still paralyzed by what his surgeon described as bruising to his spinal cord (which killed off part of it), Red's tail now wags and he's using his back thighs more and more, even jumping up a few inches for treats. The plate on his spine that was so prominent on his back, showing through his skin because he was so thin, is no longer visible. He has gained weight, his mange is gone, and he gets plenty of exercise in his cart.

Alice Louviere, the surgery technician who worked on Red, credits Red's regaining some feeling and use of his legs and tail to Diane's continued work with him. "All the massaging and movement is what got his tail moving," she said. "The fact that she kept that up is what has done it."

Despite the work it takes to keep Red clean and exercise him each day by putting him in and out of his carts (he now has four different types), Diane took on the task of caring for him with enthusiasm. She often says she needed Red as much as he needed her. She lost three family members over a three-year period, so, "Red takes care of me, too."

She took on a lot. Life for a mostly incontinent dog who weighs sixty-plus pounds means regular rinses to keep his skin clean and keep mange away, regular belly-belt changes (she has five on hand), and diaper changes throughout the day. Since Diane first adopted Red, he has graduated from his obsession with a purple squeaky toy that he treated like a baby to playing fetch with tennis balls. "If I bounce the ball, he bops up and catches it in his mouth. He can use his thighs now to jump up a little. He's too funny. He still likes his squeaky toys, but he *loves* playing ball." So they play ball several times a day, both in the house and in Diane's backyard, and take daily walks around the neighborhood with Red in a cart, one of which Diane calls his "racing car."

Life for Red couldn't be better, Diane reports. "He likes to roll on his back and flip his back legs back and forth. He wags his tail a lot more. The nerves are better. He's muscular now. He seems like a very different dog. He is doing so well. He's happy."

Peter Crowe, a volunteer from Virginia, learned a few lessons from Red. "One of the more obvious life lessons I learned from Red was to never give up and always persevere." But that, he said, was an obvious lesson for anyone who laid eyes on Red and saw his smile. "There were subtler sides to Red, both in terms of his personality and, more importantly, the things he taught us about ourselves and our own humanity." To him, Red was a symbol of "all the animals who suffered the ravages of pre- and post-Katrina times.

"Red, this sweet creature with dogfighting in his breed's lineage and his closely cropped ears," Peter said, "was clearly a caricature of his past owner's Southern macho ideas of power. By rescuing and nurturing this one special being, we were, in a sense, projecting the hopes of our rescue mission onto Red. If we could ease his suffering, spill our tears onto his forehead, and shower it with kisses, then we were, in a larger sense, putting our caring arms around and doing these same things to all of the other brave beings who suffered. If we could make him well, then we could make them all well. Only in that way could we comprehend—or better yet, be able to stomach—the scope of the awfulness of what we saw and, more importantly, what they went through. One can only hope that the wonderful final home Diane has provided for Red symbolizes and parallels what the future has in store for Katrina's other animal victims."

Red's presence on any given day at Celebration Station had a positive effect on volunteers and staffers. "After a hard day of work, we would all stream into the building, and then eat whatever someone had cooked for dinner," Peter said. Still, because of his paralysis, Red needed constant care. "One of the last things we wanted to do was clean up after the uncontrolled bowel movements of a paraplegic dog," Peter said, "no matter how sweet he was. This shared fatigue served as a sorting process, a winnowing out of the many Red admirers from the few Red devotees—those who, despite their fatigue, continued to help care for him well into the night. My interactions with Red, I shamefully admit, started as an admirer."

Peter at first assumed that one person was charged with caring for Red. "I truly thought his life was like that of the pampered lion in *The Wizard of Oz* when Dorothy's group all finally made it to the Emerald City. I was wrong. There were some very dedicated staff members who fed him and gave him his meds, and occasionally played with him, but on the whole, he spent his days stuck behind his barricade, looking for attention from anyone who would give it." Red's corner was a convalescent area for him because, with his injuries, he couldn't go into the general population of dogs.

Peter discovered a volunteer who had taken on the challenge of meeting Red's needs. "She began going into his playpen," he said, "cleaning up after his every accident, hooking him up to his chariot, and taking him for runs outside. His strength had inspired something in her, which then inspired something in me."

Once that volunteer left Celebration Station and returned home, Peter vowed to take over her self-appointed duties. "I went to Red one night and promised him that when his caretaker lady left, no matter how tired I was, I would carry her torch and take care of him as much as she had. I'm proud to say that I did so from that time on, until he was transported away from Celebration Station."

The big lesson Peter learned from Red, he said, was that "no matter how hard my day was, no matter what I had gone through, my day couldn't end as long as another being was suffering. There was no quitting bell for his suffering, so why should I be bound by one?" Red, he said, "brought out in me depths of compassion that I had never before plumbed."

One night at the center particularly stood out for him. "On that night, I had put my dinner on hold three times to clean up after his happy bladder. I then headed to the showers to clean up. When I returned, most of the place was empty, with people having gone into New Orleans or to bed. The lights were on low, and I walked over to check on Red one last time before going to bed."

Red had soiled himself again. "He was looking guiltily at me," Peter said. "His look had such a human element to it that I could have been looking at my own offspring. Since this was now the fourth time I was cleaning up his bedding, we were running very low on warm, fluffy materials, so I dug into Red's emergency stash

that I had secretly squirreled away and pulled out a soft comforter. After cleaning the plastic flooring of his excrement, I
picked him up gingerly, minding his limp legs that would criss-
cross during such lifts, set him aside, and placed his comforter in
the back corner. Then, after nesting his comforter, I again picked
him up, and laid him down as gently as I could on his new bed.

"He looked up at me with a look of love I'll never forget," Peter
continued. "I stroked his head, made sure his legs were crossed out
in front of him, then kissed him and finally retired for the night."

The next morning while Peter was at the mess table having
breakfast, a woman approached him. She said she'd watched him
the previous night from the balcony next to the sleeping area on
the second floor. "She said that she had been moved to tears by
how I had tended to Red, and, in particular, how gently I had
picked him up and then placed him into his new bed. It still
brings tears to my eyes when I think about the chain of events Red
brought about. He inspired a person, who inspired me, who
inspired and moved another person to tears—near strangers all
interacting in deeply personal ways, and all brought about by this
one beautiful being."

Red's final day at Celebration Station was sad for many, including Peter. "It was my saddest," he said. "I had heard murmurings
of his being transported out, and it was approaching the end of
February (when Celebration Station was to close), so that certainly seemed valid. But it wasn't until someone came to me in the dog
runs and told me to come say my good-byes that it hit me."

Peter walked to the back of the transport truck where a line
of people were saying farewell. "Red was sitting in his crate, looking forlorn and obviously understanding what was going on,"
Peter said. "The photos of that moment capture my unrestrained,
unabashed stream of tears. I cried. Don Arnold, the ex-Marine
trapper, cried. Dave Halperin, the original rescuer who had
responded to the initial call to rescue Red, cried. We all hugged.
This went on for thirty minutes. On his plastic crate I wrote 'We'll
miss you, Red' above his doorway, and then others followed suit,
covering his crate with expressions of love."

Volunteers and staffers signed his plastic travel crate and then sent him on his way. One person wrote "Carry on, Champ." Another, "Run like the wind, Red." Others simply penned, "I love you, Red Dog."

"I added a final message," Peter said. "Since Red was going to a rescue shelter in Texas, I wrote 'Don't mess with Red' in big red letters."

Red, Peter said, did more than inspire volunteers with his "never quit" personality. "He helped to bring out the best, the most compassionate parts of a human," he explained, "and then enabled us to share these deeply personal emotions with near strangers. Finally, he taught us that whatever limitations we imagine we have are all in our heads. What better test of the greatness of a being than this?"

11

Fifteen Minutes of Fame

W E'VE LOST EVERYTHING, MOM," twelve-year-old Nicholas Willheit told his mother after the family realized they wouldn't be returning to their house in Chalmette anytime soon. "I lost my friends. I lost my things. All I want back is my dog."

Julie Willheit searched the Internet for hours each night trying to find Cujo's photo on rescue sites, all in an effort to bring her son's dog home to him. "Nicholas and Cujo grew up together," Julie said. "Nicholas was my inspiration to find Cujo."

Eventually, Nicholas stopped talking about Cujo. So on a winter afternoon in November, more than two months after Hurricane Katrina, the last thing Nicholas thought he would see was his nine-year-old terrier-and-Poodle mix.

Julie and her family were staying with friends, and each night Julie logged onto her friend's computer, searching for a photo of Cujo and sending e-mails about him to rescue groups, including Best Friends, which had rescued him. A positive match was made, and Julie was put in touch with Cujo's foster mom, with whom he'd been living in North Carolina since late September. They arranged to meet in Baytown, Texas.

That day, Julie and her daughter drove to pick up Cujo. "When we pulled up, my daughter saw a van with the words 'Katrina Rescue' on the side. She started crying," Julie said. "The woman was standing waiting for us, and Cujo was in the van in the front seat. I said his name—we call him Cujie. Right when I did that, he whipped around and started jumping over [the woman], trying to get to us."

When they put him in the car to take him home, "we were loving him to death. He was still thin. We bought him a ten-piece nugget meal and drove home."

Nicholas was playing in a football game that afternoon in Spring, Texas, so Julie drove her daughter and Cujo to the ball field. Before the game, Julie took the coach aside and told him they were planning to surprise her son after the game with his dog. "Let me handle it," the coach told her.

At the end of the game, Nicholas's coach stopped him from walking off the field. "Wait a minute, Nicholas," the coach said into a microphone. "We have a special prize for you." Nicholas thought it was because his team had won the game and he was being singled out for playing well.

"Look!" the coach said as he pointed toward one of the goal posts at the end of the field. Nicholas turned to see what his coach was pointing at. There, standing beside Randy Willheit, Nicholas's father, was a dog.

It couldn't be, Nicholas thought. Then he knew. "Cujo!" the boy yelled. The dog ran across the field toward Nicholas, and Nicholas ran toward his dog. When they reached each other, Nicholas dropped to his knees and Cujo jumped up and began licking his face.

The coach explained the reunion to the spectators in the stand. "The whole stadium was crying," Julie said. Since the storm, the Willheits have moved back to the New Orleans area, but this time to Mandeville, north of Lake Pontchartrain, in a house on two and a half acres. "Cujo gets to run around on the property, and he loves it," Julie said.

It had been two and a half long months since the Willheits had left Cujo at the Chalmette Medical Center, where Julie worked before the storm. Julie's husband and adult daughter, along with Cujo and a little Chihuahua named ChiChi, rode out the storm. Nicholas had evacuated earlier with his grandmother.

When they learned they'd have to leave their dogs behind, Julie was beside herself. An army pilot had landed a helicopter on the roof and was evacuating people to the airport. "It was the people running the hospital, and not the army, who made the decision. They told us we couldn't take our animals."

She took a risk keeping ChiChi with her, but ChiChi was small enough to fit in her bag. "I grabbed her, took her blanket, her toy, and a little bit of food I had left, put her in my bag, and zipped it up. When I sat down in the helicopter, it was so loud no one knew, but I kept thinking, *They'll find out and take her from me.*" When Julie sat down in the chopper, her husband wasn't happy and said he was afraid they'd be kicked off. "I told him, 'Then I'll get off the helicopter. I'll stay if I have to. I'm not leaving her. I'll take my chances.' "

Cujo was too big to hide, so they had to leave him on the roof with Dennis Rizzuto and the other pets. Dennis, a generous man they had never before met, had volunteered to hand out food at the hospital, and he offered to stay behind and care for Cujo and several other dogs whose owners had gathered there. He told the pets' owners that he would take the dogs to his Evangeline Street apartment when the water subsided and care for them until the families returned. He gave them all his address and phone number. "When Cujo was walked up the hospital ramp and handed to that man, Cujo looked back at me like he was saying, 'Why aren't you coming?' It's such a bad decision for people to have to make. It's something no pet owner should ever have to go through."

After the helicopter landed at the airport, someone from Delta approached the Willheits to say a flight was leaving and pointed to where they should stand in line. "I still had ChiChi in the bag," Julie said. "I was so scared they'd find her. I kept peeking in and putting water in a bottle cap for her. We stood in line for a while. Finally, I just pulled one of the flight attendants to the side. I said, 'I have a dog.' He said, 'Where is it?' I showed him. He looked at me and said, 'You can hold her. That's not an issue.' He said to take her out of the bag so they could search it. 'You might as well take her out now,' the flight attendant told me.

Everybody on the flight fell in love with her. They took pictures of us. When we boarded, they told me I didn't have to put her back in the bag." The CEO of Delta was on the flight, and he gave her a dog biscuit from his coat pocket. "Right then," Julie said, "my heart was saying, 'Here, everybody is fine with her, and I was forced to leave Cujo. They would have been okay with him, too.'"

The flight took them to Georgia. "When we came off the flight, reporters were there," she said. "CNN interviewed us." Julie's family, who hadn't yet heard from her, saw Julie walking off the plane holding her Chihuahua.

When the Willheits went to Dennis's apartment three weeks after the storm, the dogs were already gone. Dennis was, too. They left a note telling Dennis they were looking for Cujo, included their number, and wrote that they were in Texas. They didn't even know if Dennis would be returning to the apartment. Julie was beside herself, not knowing what had happened to Cujo. She later learned that five days after Dennis took the pets to his building, he was ordered by police to leave the flood-damaged area.

Unknown to the Willheits and the other pet guardians at the time was that Best Friends had rescued their dogs ten days after Dennis evacuated. A *Dateline NBC* crew had been with the team on September 15 filming the rescue. After the *Dateline* special about Best Friends' rescues aired on Sunday, September 18, viewers called in to say they'd recognized their missing pets. As a result, those rescued and reunited included Cujo and other dogs—Tiny, Tinkerbelle, Ketel, Son, Buttons, and Agustas—and also a cat named Bubba, whose reunion was filmed by the *Dateline* crew.

Bart Siegal never thought he'd see his cats again. Bart lived just a couple of blocks from where the first levees were breeched, and his living room filled to the ceiling in just ten minutes. He and his daughter made it to the roof with their two cats, Bubba and Bugsy. A rescue boat with the U.S. Fish and Wildlife Service picked them up a day later and took them to a bank in Chalmette, where they stayed for four days. When he and his daughter were evacuated from the bank, Bart was told that he couldn't take his cats with him.

Forced to leave, Bart left Bubba and Bugsy in a second-floor office. As soon as he arrived at a rescue center in Dallas, he had people send out pleas for someone to retrieve his cats from the Regions Bank on Judge Perez Drive. That's where Best Friends and the *Dateline* crew found Bubba. Unfortunately, Bugsy, who had diabetes, didn't make it.

Bart had left a note with the cats. Rob Stafford, a correspondent in the field with NBC that day, read the note and then sent an SOS message to his NBC newsroom for help. NBC employees, in turn, were able to locate Bart's mother on the People Finder online search engine. Bart's mother, after being called by *Dateline*, notified her son, who was staying in a Dallas hotel, that Bubba had been rescued. Bart, who had lost everything he owned, rented a car and drove ten hours through the night to Camp Tylertown to retrieve his long-haired gray cat. Rob, who ended up fostering a Katrina dog he'd helped rescue, was at Camp Tylertown with his film crew to videotape the reunion.

Tiny and Tinkerbelle were reunited, too, but with their owner's mother, not with the man who had raised them. Their person, David Carruthers, returned to New Orleans only to find that his two small dogs were gone and his house had been destroyed. As the storm was about to hit and just before he evacuated, he'd put his two dogs in a boat that was tied to a tree in his front yard. He had no way of knowing that the boat would later drift off. It ended up a couple of blocks away, landing on debris in the yard of the Evangeline apartment building, from which the Best Friends team retrieved his dogs.

David was devastated by the loss—so much so that he took his own life by hanging himself from the same tree. His dogs, however, did find their way home. The day after David's death, his mother received a phone call from a former neighbor telling her that he'd watched the *Dateline NBC* segment and recognized Tiny and Tinkerbelle being rescued.

David's dogs, who had been placed in separate foster homes after their rescue, were returned to base camp. Two weeks later, David's mother, Karen Burns-Carruthers, drove to Camp Tyler-town to pick up Tinkerbelle, a West Highland White Terrier, and Tiny, a Chihuahua. Karen called it a miracle to have located her son's dogs.

A Cocker Spaniel mix named Agustas was in foster care as well. When his people saw him on TV, they, too, notified Best Friends and were put in touch with the New Hampshire foster home that had been taking care of Agustas, and he was returned.

Annette Gilligan learned what had happened to her Maltese, Ketel, and her parents' Boston Terrier, Son, when she received an excited phone call on a Sunday night. "I just saw my dog on TV," her mother squealed into the phone. She had also seen Annette's dog, but Annette was skeptical. Her mother couldn't tell her the name of the show, just that she remembered that the animal group was Best Friends.

The Saturday before Hurricane Katrina touched down on land, Annette's mother had gone to work at Chalmette Medical Center in St. Bernard Parish. Annette had left Ketel with her parents for a visit. The next day, Annette's father joined his wife at the hospital.

"On the Sunday before the storm, my father packed up the dogs, Ketel and Son, and took them with him to the hospital to ride out the storm with my mother," Annette said. On Monday, the hurricane hit. "No one ever imagined the actual damage Katrina would do. At four thirty a.m. I was evacuated to Baton Rouge and watched the coverage with friends."

The storm "took the homes of every family member I have and, for six weeks, it took my two dogs, too. The past three and a half years of my life have been spent with an eight-pound Maltese named Ketel who has been not just my pet, but my baby as well."

Her parents had been trapped at the hospital, where the water had risen to ten feet. "They had generators, food, and medical staff, but no escape," she said. The dogs stayed in a hospital room with them. A few days later, a military helicopter landed on the roof to begin evacuating the medical center. Annette's parents packed one bag with clothes and left the other empty for stowing Ketel and Son, and then they headed for the roof. Once there, however, they were told "No dogs allowed" by hospital personnel, just as Julie Willheit had been. Ketel and Son became two more pets Dennis Rizzuto agreed to look after.

Annette later picked up her parents from Louis Armstrong New Orleans International Airport, and that's when she learned the bad news. Her mother cried when she told her daughter about how they were forced to leave Son and Ketel. Annette immediately registered both dogs on the Petfinder Web site and went twice to the Lamar-Dixon shelter looking for them. She drove to Noah's Wish in Slidell and the Louisiana SPCA shelters. They weren't there. So, when her mother called her and said she had just seen the dogs on TV, Annette didn't believe it. Her mother insisted, however, that she'd seen them being carried out of Dennis's apartment building by two men. She was right. Ethan Gurney and Jeff Popowich, members of Best Friends rapid response team, had been videotaped rescuing Son and Ketel.

Annette tracked down Best Friends to its base camp in Tylertown, Mississippi, and drove there with her mother in search of their dogs. They were shown photos and information about pets in both the rescue center's database and in binders. There, Annette's mother saw photos not only of Ketel and Son, but also of a dog named Buttons who belonged to Annette's friend. They learned that the three had been fostered out to different homes, and arrangements would be made to return them to Camp Tylertown.

In the meantime, they called their friends the Dominos to let them know that Buttons had been rescued and had been placed in a nearby foster home in McComb, Mississippi.

As soon as Annette got the call that her Maltese and her parents' Boston Terrier were being flown in a private plane by Best Friends staffer Juliette Watt—back to Camp Tylertown from foster care in Chicago—she sped to Mississippi to meet them.

Back home in Gonzales, Louisiana, Ketel and Son appear unscathed from the ordeal. "They're fine and as spoiled as ever," Annette said in a phone interview. "It's like they were on holiday the whole time." Her advice for those who lose pets is simple: "Keep looking. Don't give up."

Sal Domino, who picked up Buttons a few days later, credited his dog with keeping him alive after his bypass surgery months earlier. During the hurricane, Sal and his wife, Joan, along with Buttons (so named because she chewed the buttons off Sal's shirts), stayed at the Chalmette hospital, where Joan worked as a housekeeping supervisor. After they were evacuated and had to leave Buttons, Sal's world fell apart. He was grieving for his dog.

Once the family relocated to Tickpaw, Louisiana, they began their search for Buttons, but without any luck. They went to the Louisiana Humane Society and to Chalmette High School, where animals also were being kept, then to the large temporary shelter in Gonzales, and finally to Tylertown. Sal didn't believe he was going to get Buttons back until he saw her being carried to him by her foster mom, Sarah Booker, a veterinary technician who had driven her to base camp from her home a few miles away in McComb. According to Sal, Buttons meant the world to him. He had given up, telling his wife that was the last trip he would make to look for Buttons. His search was over. As a crowd of volunteers stood by, Buttons licked Sal's face when she first saw him. Sal was overcome with emotion. His family said having Buttons back in Sal's life made all the difference. She gave him a reason to live.

12

The Twister Sisters

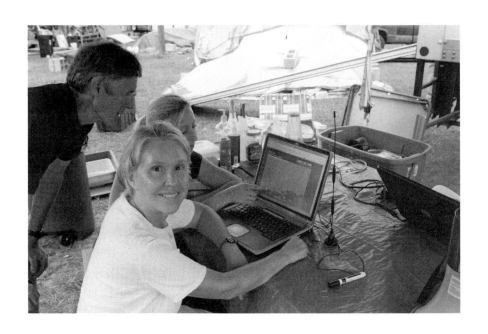

O N SEPTEMBER 24, HURRICANE RITA touched down on the Louisiana-Texas border. Because of the landing's close proximity to Mississippi, volunteers at Camp Tylertown battened down and prepared for the possibility of a hurricane.

Professional stormchasers Peggy Willenberg, from Plymouth, Minnesota, and her partner Melanie Trockman, from nearby St. Cloud, were at Camp Tylertown to record the storm. Peggy and Melanie are known as the Twister Sisters. Two National Geographic documentaries have aired segments about the pair's storm-chasing antics. They follow storms for Fox News, Channel 9, in Minneapolis, where they report on severe weather from April through August, traveling and chasing along the way during tornado season.

The two had planned to volunteer, not as storm experts, but just like any other volunteer—until Hurricane Rita was about to make landfall. As the weather changed for the worse, they set up their computer equipment and created a mini–storm central at base camp. Studying storm data on their laptop computer under a tarp, they provided reports every fifteen minutes as volunteers and staffers staked in all the kennels, tightening down everything that could be picked up and blown about.

By afternoon, a dark, ominous cloud rolled in and hovered nearby. That, the Twister Sisters explained, was the edge of the storm.

Five hundred plastic igloos had been delivered the day before—straw was placed inside for bedding—to shelter the dogs from thirty-mile-an-hour wind gusts. Igloos were placed in each run for every animal. Everybody kicked into high gear as workers buttoned up, battened down, and prepared for the possibility of Hurricane Rita bearing down on the Best Friends relief center. While the Twister Sisters did their thing, other volunteers broke down tents, removed tarps from kennels, and picked up anything in the yard that could become a projectile. As the day progressed and the storm mass shadowed base camp, the dogs took cover inside their new igloos. The smallest dogs, those in Toytown, were taken inside the three bungalows on the property, and volunteers who'd been sleeping in tents moved inside and prepared to sleep on the floor.

By afternoon, photographer Clay Myers, who doubled as a maintenance repairman when needed, was working on the roof of an RV where four staffers slept, fastening something that was about to blow away. I ran over to where he was working with his back to the cloud and shouted against the wind, "Clay, look up!" as I pointed toward the incoming cloud. "Wow!" he shouted back. He made his way to a ladder, climbed down from the RV, grabbed his camera gear from indoors, and shot photos of Rita.

That day's rescue crew, on their way to St. Bernard Parish, was called back, just to be on the safe side, because Hurricane Rita was forecast to hit New Orleans hard. The dogs and cats at base camp were restless, so volunteers sat with them to help calm them. Then everyone hoped for the best and waited as the winds picked up and clouds emptied over Camp Tylertown. Throughout the night, rain poured and wind lashed, and it sounded like the roofs of the bungalows were being ripped apart. Some runs filled with water in the middle of the night, and volunteers and staffers, fighting the wind and rain, moved the dogs to runs that hadn't flooded.

Volunteers packed into the loft above the main building—a laundry room and cattery with a kitchen and a bathroom—to get out of the storm. I slept on the floor in the office, as usual, with my foster Chihuahuas Lois Lane and Mia shivering with fear as they hid under the covers, cringing in their smallness from something so big. They seemed sure the storm was going to get them. And it sounded like it would, especially in the middle of the night when the storm seemed the worst. I imagined the dogs in their igloos must have thought that Hurricane Katrina was bearing down on them once again as it rattled their plastic shelters. The wind tearing at the roof sounded like it was going to rip it away.

Peggy and Melanie—who in reality are friends and not sisters—braved the storm in their tent along with a few other daring campers. Everyone else at camp had taken cover elsewhere, either inside a building or in cars and campers. Peggy and Melanie camped on the grass, sleeping through Rita. By daybreak, their tent was the only one that hadn't been damaged by the torrential rain and winds.

Although small items had been scattered about camp, most everything else had stayed intact. No one, including the animals, was hurt.

The people and pets of New Orleans didn't fare as well. It took a week to pump dry the newly flooded areas left in Rita's wake, leading to more pets being displaced and causing more damage to homes.

Surprisingly, Rita had a silver lining. When the storm blew away, she took with her swarms of love bugs, providing a welcome relief from the billions that had taken up residence in the region. Before Rita, the amorous flies—dipterans, also known as June bugs, that form large, dense swarms—thickened the air around Camp Tylertown. They were everywhere and landed on just about everything, forming a black blanket and claiming every object—including food—as their territory. We had to be careful not to breathe too deeply while outside or we'd capture a mouthful.

Love-bug mating season was in full swing, and the air and everything they landed on was thick with the buggers for what seemed an eternity. Hurricane Rita, in her vigor, carried them all away.

13

Other Homeless Critters

RESCUE TEAMS MADE TREACHEROUS TREKS through sewage and diesel-contaminated floodwaters to retrieve not only dogs and cats, but also pot-bellied pigs, birds, geese, ducks, turtles, snakes, exotic fish, tarantulas, ferrets, and an emu left stranded by the storm. Regardless of their species, all kinds of animals were rescued from the streets of New Orleans and taken to the Tylertown base camp.

A tiny Muskogee duckling was found in mid-September, swimming in a pond with two other ducks. A team, including volunteers Rochelle Fraser and Jeremy Glover, dog handler John Garcia, and two volunteer veterinarians, was searching St. Bernard Parish for pets when they spotted a house that was spray-painted with the words "Cat in Garage" and "Ducks Out Back." The team walked to the back of the house. "There they were," said Rochelle. "Three ducks swimming in this dirty pond. Someone had left them a big bag of dog food opened and on the shore." Two white ducks "and this little ugly duckling were swimming. The duckling didn't look anything like the other two. The vets said they needed to look at him. He didn't look very healthy. He was small and spotted and pretty dirty."

It took a good hour to round them up. "If you've ever seen a bunch of animal lovers try to catch a duck, it's hilarious," she said. "We threw rocks in the opposite direction of where they were swimming to see if they would swim the other way." It worked. "Whichever way we tossed the rocks, they swam the other way. One walked out of the water, and we put him in a crate." To lure the others, they carried the crate, with the duck inside, to the edge of the water. "He started squawking, and the other two walked up to the crate. We put them all in the van in the large crate. They stood up and looked at us through the wire door."

With the ducks safely in the van, the team opened the garage door to rescue the cat. "The cat meowed and came right to us," Rochelle said. "He was in pretty good shape. Someone had left him food in the garage." It felt good to rescue the four, Rochelle said, because earlier in the day they'd gone to a property where several horses and dogs hadn't made it. "It was the most ghastly thing I'd ever seen." She remembers one of the team members saying, "There's nothing we can do for them. We need to get out of here and rescue." They happened to turn down one particular street, and that's when they spotted the words painted on the house about the ducks and the cat.

That night, they arrived at base camp with the rescued animals. Mary Lichtenberger, a volunteer from Ohio who handled intake and foster paperwork, was there for the baby duck's arrival. Mary, who knew how to care for ducks because she'd had one for ten years, made a makeshift habitat for the duckling in a large crate in the laundry room in Kitty City. The laundry area, which also served as a grooming room, was the entrance to the building, so volunteers going in and out became all too familiar with the vocal duckling. Everyone called him Ducky. He made sure to greet everyone who walked through the door by flapping his wings and making noises, but he didn't quack. The sounds emanating from that duckling are difficult to describe, but whatever he was trying to say, he said it with gusto.

Mary exercised him at least twice a day by filling a large sink with water so he could splash around and swim. Ducky vigorously flapped his featherless wings, which looked like fuzzy pink sticks because he was still a baby. But he splashed around in the water like he was a full-grown duck. After his baths, he sat wrapped in a towel on volunteers' laps as they input computer data. He seemed to enjoy it.

But Ducky was growing fast, tripling in size in just six weeks. It became obvious that he needed to be around his own kind, so he was fostered out to a couple who had fifty other domestic ducks and geese just outside of Becker, Minnesota. Soon, he was all grown up and doing well at the twenty-acre hobby farm, swimming in ponds and splashing around in mud areas with other ducks. He was named Louis after his native Louisiana. Once it was determined that "he" was a "she," however, the duckling was quickly renamed Louise. From the start, Louise's new best friend at the hobby farm was a young Guinea hen named Pop. When Louise went into the water, Pop was close behind, but the hen soon realized he wasn't a duck when he nearly drowned. Like a big brother, Pop watched over Louise, regularly running interference with the geese stepping in her path.

Louise's diet in her new digs is similar to the food she grew up on—spinach, tomatoes, hard-boiled eggs, and fruit. Now, she also regularly eats cantaloupe, grapes, and watermelon, with bread and lettuce as treats. In addition, just like when she was living in Camp Tylertown, Louise still eats cracked corn and oats. During the warmer months, she swims in a one-acre pond. Her favorite activity, according to the farm operators, is diving for peas as they sink in the pond water. Her once-sparse feathers have grown iridescent, and her guardians report that she's both beautiful *and* happy.

Other birds arrived at Camp Tylertown, too, including a half dozen chickens rescued in late September from a hiding place behind coolers at a Chevron station on Chef Menteur Highway in Gentilly. Their rescuers reported that it appeared they were being fed, possibly by residents who had returned to the area. The chickens—which were a mixture of red, white, and black in color—were eventually placed in a foster home in Bellevue, Colorado, on a large piece of property.

Out of the sundry pets arriving at base camp, perhaps the most challenging to care for were the tarantulas, especially the large ones. Cherie Fox, a veterinary technician from Ohio, took charge of them for a few days, and just before her stint was up, a replacement caregiver was sought. Best Friends issued a request on the Internet: "Arachnophiliac volunteer needed!! The kind volunteer who's been taking care of the tarantulas at our St. Francis Sanctuary at Tylertown will shortly have to leave. If you are an arachnophiliac and can take her place for a while, please fill out this form and specify that you are willing to help with the tarantulas. Thanks!"

Fifteen spiders, including a variety of tarantulas, had taken up residence at the relief center. They too were left behind in the wake of Hurricane Katrina, rescued, and driven to Camp Tylertown. The two largest tarantulas were picked up from an apartment on Washington Avenue in the Garden District of New Orleans. The team noted on the admissions paperwork that each spider had two big fangs. Another batch of tarantulas arrived in the tin cans that they'd lived in at one home. Volunteer Susie Duttge helped transfer them—very carefully—from the cans to larger, aquarium-like housing. "The owner had them stuffed into tiny containers," she said, "which showed that even tarantulas can suffer from animal abuse. A lot of them were dead in those containers. The bigger ones survived. We used bottle caps from the gallon water jugs as water bowls. They eat live crickets, and somehow those were located for them." Caring for tarantulas, Susie said, "is not too eventful once you get them set up in their home. Water and crickets is about it."

Meanwhile, during her turn caring for the spiders, Cherie Fox busily got up to speed on the care and feeding of tarantulas. She pulled an all-nighter when the first group of spiders arrived, making sure they all took in water. Cherie used potting soil as substrate for what she described as "their clean new homes," which were close to a natural environment. "They're acting very lively," she reported after the first day.

The names of the species believed to be at base camp were a mouthful: Brachypelma, grammostola aureastriata, grammostola pulchra, aphonopelma moderatum, aphonopelma coloradanum, aphonopelma Borelli, and aphonopelma chalcodes.

After a story about the tarantulas ran on the Web, many readers provided tips and even offered to take them in. They congratulated the rescuers for "saving such misunderstood critters." One person thanked Cherie specifically for "helping the scared, innocent spiders." Another reader commented, "Pigs, a squirrel, an emu, an iguana, and now tarantulas—oh, my!" Soon the tarantulas were transported to the able hands of an experienced tarantula keeper at a zoo in Alabama. Juliette Watt, a volunteer coordinator for Best Friends who happens to be a pilot with a four-seater plane, flew the tarantula passengers to their new habitat.

For the caregivers at the camp, even more challenging than the spiders was an emu, a large Australian ostrichlike bird. It wasn't just basic care that was a challenge; also in question was where to put him so he would be both safe and comfortable.

The emu had been rescued on September 17 near the Murphy Oil refinery, where the storm caused more than twenty-five thousand barrels of crude oil to be released into the towns of Meraux and Chalmette just two and a half weeks earlier. The emu, whom volunteers called Big Bird, was noticed as he walked in a ditch near the railroad tracks parallel to St. Bernard Highway just past the refinery. "We couldn't believe it," said Dana Herman, a volunteer from Minnesota, who was with a team that included Dr. Will Magum, a veterinarian from Atlanta; Ken Ray, a volunteer and animal control officer from Alabama; and Chipa Wolfe, a volunteer from Georgia who had experience with wildlife. The team split up, with Dana, Will, and Ken in the transport vehicle—the large air-conditioned cargo van dubbed "the Big Nasty" after black dirt from the streets was tracked into it.

"We were driving on St. Bernard Highway, and the emu was walking along the fence line," Dana said. "We could see a ship, maybe a military ship, behind him. There was a big fence that ran alongside the road, and the emu was in a ditch following the

A volunteer comforts a just-rescued kitten named Love Bug.

Craig Hill, a volunteer from New Jersey, searches for surviving pets in a storm-damaged house in the Lower Ninth Ward.

A house with a standard "X" from rescuers indicating the remains of a dog on a leash who died on the porch.

An unnamed volunteer walks rescued dogs from a St. Bernard Parish street to a waiting van with fellow rescuers John Hoenemeier (center) and Ethan Gurney (right).

Angel, a Pit Bull, just after she was rescued from the second floor of St. Bernard High School.

Rescuer John Hoenemeier lures a cat from his hiding place.

Mike McCleese from
Cincinnati carries an
exhausted terrier mix
to a transport van in
St. Bernard Parish.

A frightened dog flees in a damaged Gentilly neighborhood.

A lost spaniel-Beagle mix watches as he's about to be rescued.

A terrier mix slips from his hiding place under a house.

Kelli Orhtman and fellow rescuer Doug Klein feed a just-rescued German Shepherd mix. The dog, named Sandy, was later reunited with her family.

A kitten (later named Nola Vie) is rescued from Plaquemines Parish in November 2005.

A frightened Pit Bull mix (later named Bright Eyes) watches as rescuers approach his hiding place.

Rescuer Ethan Gurney gives Bright Eyes a treat.

Lane Ikenberry pets his cat, Petey, at their damaged home
in Orleans Parish.

Volunteer Suzanne "Trixie"
Hall carries an injured dog
to safety at Plaquemines
Parish.

Police K-9 handler Cliff Deutsch carries BayBay, an English Cocker Spaniel, to safety.

A cat walks a storm-damaged street three weeks after the hurricane.

Sheriff, a scared and hungry Rottweiler, stares as his rescuers approach.

A cat is captured in a humane trap in a damaged Gentilly neighborhood.

Janice Tuma walks a Beagle she just rescued from a street in Violet,
in St. Bernard Parish.

Dr. Debbie Rykoff hydrates an injured dog as veterinary technician Jeff Popowich and Suzanne "Trixie" Hall assist.

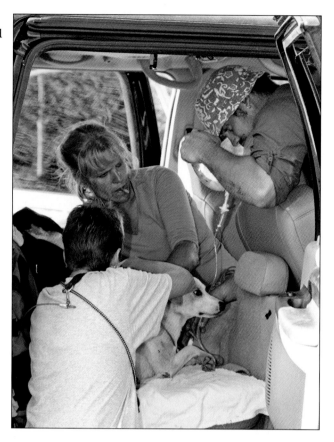

Volunteer Kim Johnson points out on a map where feeding and water stations are set up for stranded pets.

An aerial view of the grounds at St. Francis Animal Sanctuary's fifty acres in Tylertown, Mississippi.

Sean Scherer (front, with Beagle) and fellow volunteers in the admissions area at Camp Tylertown.

Volunteers wet down an overheated Jack Russell Terrier at base camp.

Groomer Laura Loder cleans up a rescued Maltese at base camp.

Drying food dishes in the Back Forty area at Camp Tylertown.

A volunteer watches over sleeping puppies at the Celebration Station triage center.

Michael Mountain, president of Best Friends Animal Society, gets up close and personal with Big Bird, an emu rescued from St. Bernard Parish.

A rescued Beagle greets a visitor at Celebration Station's triage center in Metairie, a suburb of New Orleans.

Volunteers (left to right) Catherine "Cat" Gabrel, Tom Gambill, and Kelli Ohrtman on the porch at the M*A*S*H Unit triage area at Camp Tylertown.

Hurricane Rita hovers over Camp Tylertown.

Volunteer caregiver Bob Rude pauses with a young cat at base camp's Kitty City.

Susan Thomas takes a break next to a transport van with a just-rescued dog from the streets of New Orleans.

A volunteer's bedding and cot below her native Canadian flag, on the second floor in the sleeping quarters of the Celebration Station triage center.

Chandra Sigmund, who helped run the cat triage center at Celebration Station, works at night with a rescued cat on her lap.

Cofounders Pam Perez (left) and Heidi Krupp (right) on the grounds of St. Francis Animal Sanctuary in Tylertown, home to base camp, with their rescued yellow Labs.

Volunteer veterinary technician Carey Belcher makes the rounds in Kitty City on Christmas Eve.

Animal expert Sherry Woodard holds a puppy in a stocking on Christmas Day at Camp Tylertown.

A rescued dog at base camp carries a Christmas present: a PVC pipe stuffed with wet dog food.

Itty Bitty, an aging two-and-a-half-pound Chihuahua, at base camp shortly after her rescue.

Adopter Diane McDermott walks behind her Boynton Beach, Florida, home with Red, a paralyzed Pit Bull rescued after the storm.

Myra and Michael Burchell hug their Yorkshire Terrier, Rosco, at base camp when they see him for the first time after the storm.

Connie Fitch playing at home with BayBay (featured on this book's cover) after the English Cocker Spaniel was rescued from a flooded backyard shed.

The Hurtado family reunite with their Boxers, Kassi and Uggio, as animal care manager Sherry Woodard looks on.

Sadie, a Chow Chow, and John David at his New Orleans flower shop after their reunion.

Allen Thomas and Buddy at home after they're reunited.

A bald Poodle, dubbed the "Survivor" and later named Marina, tries to hide just before she's rescued.

Marina, the formerly bald Poodle, being cradled a year later by her adopter, Mary Salter.

fence line. I said, 'What the hell did we just see?' Dr. Will said he knew all about emus and that we should pick him up. Somebody radioed Chipa, and he came in with his pickup. With their arms, they corralled this emu and walked him back to the Big Nasty."

But it was tougher than it sounded. The emu wore them out. "The poor thing didn't know where he was," said Chipa, who rescues wildlife at home in Georgia. "I'd had a couple of emus that people brought to my farm, and I've wrestled with an emu before. They can take their toes and cut you up." Chipa, who has a reputation for being a gentle animal handler, intended to catch Big Bird without harming himself or the emu.

On top of not having had any food for nearly three weeks, the emu was frightened. With Ken nearby, Chipa slowly approached the emu and then tried to grab him.

"The only way I know to move an emu is, once you've caught him, grab his neck and put your arm over his back to stabilize him," he said, "otherwise he'll beat you with his head and hurt himself in the process."

That's what Chipa started to do. "I threw my arm over his back," he said. But what happened next took Chipa by surprise.

"All of a sudden, the emu put one foot up and kicked me right into the chain-link fence," he said. "I bounced right back. It was like a cartoon." Chipa was unhurt, and he and Ken began guiding the emu, who by that time had calmed down. They walked him, holding his neck, toward the van parked on the deserted road. Once there, they picked up the bird and put him inside.

Dr. Will stood with the emu in the aisle between kennels in the back of the van to make sure he didn't harm himself in such close quarters. The kennels inside the van were half full at that point with rescued dogs and cats.

"They gave him water, and Dr. Will tried to keep him calm during the three-hour drive back to Mississippi," Chipa said.

It was a good day for the pets stranded in St. Bernard Parish. "We caught a menagerie that day," Chipa said. "I got three pythons. One was a rock python inside somebody's house. Because it was dark inside the house, he looked just like a moccasin snake. I had to grab his head in the dark. I got a ball python from somebody's boat. It was stuck in a fisherman's net, and it was cutting into the end of the snake. I got him out." Besides the emu and three pythons, the team rescued thirty dogs, fifteen cats, a three-foot iguana, and the first pot-bellied pig from the streets that day.

At Camp Tylertown, the emu was fed and housed in a large run near the entrance to the second gate. The next challenge was to transport the bird to a sanctuary. The Big Nasty van was used for transport only from New Orleans to base camp, so other transportation needed to be found. A zoological society had agreed to take the bird, but the workers at Camp Tylertown had to find a vehicle tall enough to fit the long-necked emu comfortably. A volunteer ended up pulling him in a horse trailer nine hundred miles to his new home at the Racine Zoo in Wisconsin. Big Bird, when he arrived, had some medical issues and was dehydrated. Today, however, the zoo reports that Big Bird—now named Perth—is doing well and is nicer than typical emus, who have a tendency to be defensive.

"He has a girlfriend and has had one for some time," said Eric Hileman, a director at the zoo. "He gets along really well with her. He's got a sweet disposition."

The emu was put in a standard quarantine for thirty days, but because he still had some medical problems, he remained in quarantine until early December 2005. "He was in pretty rough shape when we first got him," Eric said. "He wouldn't eat, and he wouldn't defecate initially. We assumed he was a pet and that he had been fed inappropriate foods for an emu. Initially we tried to give him the food he should have. He was not consuming his diet, so it was several days before we started giving him bread and other things he would have had as a pet. We slowly got him to eat food for emus."

In November of that year, Perth underwent a deworming series, but in the meantime tested positive for what Eric described as "a pretty nasty parasite." With time, however, the emu showed signs of improvement. By December 5, his tests were clean, and three days later he was placed in an exhibit on zoo property. The *Racine Journal-Times* published a story about the emu who had arrived from New Orleans. As yet, though, there's no signage informing visitors to the zoo that Perth is a hurricane survivor. When the signs at his habitat are in need of replacing, Eric said, they'll include Perth's background.

Meanwhile, Perth's good health continues. He's nesting, and zookeepers expect his female emu companion to lay fertilized eggs in the near future. "He's in great shape now," Eric said. "He adjusted fairly rapidly. He's in our Walk-about Creek. It's one of the largest exhibits here. He's in there with kangaroos and does very well with them." The zoo is located on thirty-two acres on the shores of Lake Michigan. With just two hundred animals, Eric said, the zoo is able to have large habitats, such as the one Perth lives in.

When asked if it's unusual for a zoo to take in an exotic bird that's been a pet most of his life, he said, "We knew he was in trouble, and we knew we were in a position to take him. We had a great opportunity here to save one life. We had space that was already available. All of our zookeepers here are in it because they're passionate and care about the animals' well-being."

Camp Tylertown was also beginning to resemble a zoo. Besides the pig picked up the same day as the emu in St. Bernard Parish, a rescue team took in two other pot-bellied pigs. A large black one called Raisin by volunteers was found near a school and was suffering from dog bites. He was treated and then, like Big Bird, relocated to the Racine Zoo in Wisconsin.

Volunteers doted on Raisin during his stay at Camp Tylertown. Jan Martin, a veterinary technician from Orange County, California, got to know Raisin as she made her rounds around the animal areas. "There was some hay in his run," Jan said. "The pig would bury himself underneath the hay. I'd call the pig, and he would come over to the fence and put his hoofs up on the chain link. I'd put my hand through and pet him. He was friendly."

Raisin was treated at the M*A*S*H Unit before moving to Wisconsin. "We kept the pig through quarantine," Eric Hileman, director of the Racine Zoo, said. "We didn't have accommodations for him here." Raisin, once he recovered from his ordeal and was in good enough health to travel, was transferred to a different zoo in Wisconsin, where he now lives.

Back at base camp one evening, volunteer Vicki Schutt from Minnesota was headed to her tent not far from the Heights, where many of the larger dogs were kept. She saw Susie, a 250-pound pig, slowly making her way down one of the grassy aisles between the dog runs, taking herself for a walk. Vicki put a loop leash around Susie's neck, but the pig, who barely had a neck, slipped out. Not knowing what else to do, Vicki hollered out, "Loose pig!" and several people at camp soon corralled Susie back to her own pen in the dog barn.

Susie and the unnamed third pig eventually went to Jo Dawn Farms, a petting zoo in Franksville, Wisconsin. A representative from Jo Dawn Farms said the pigs were doing well and had adjusted to their new home.

Angel Parker, a New Orleans resident, was missing a green iguana. It was probably one of the oddest, yet most touching, reunions to come out of the rescues because Angel had a most unusual combination of pets.

After she was notified that her animals were at Camp Tylertown, Angel drove with her children in their SUV to base camp. A couple of weeks earlier, as she and her family were about to be evacuated, she'd left her eight pets with a friend. The friend, however, was forced to evacuate and, in turn, handed Angel's pets over to the Jefferson Parish Animal Shelter. On a routine trip back from New Orleans, Best Friends stopped at the shelter and picked up the group, along with paperwork that identified Angel as the pets' guardian.

Angel's brood was quite a collection. She was reunited on an October evening with her entire gang of pets, which included an iguana named Heineken, a Pit Bull called Cornbread, a Rottweiler named Mary Jane, and Miko the Maltese, not to mention four cats—Oddball, Alicia, Sassy, and Pretty Boy. Volunteers, who looked forward each day to reunions, grabbed their cameras and surrounded Angel as her pets, one by one, were brought to her. When her iguana, Heineken, was handed to her, she kissed its face, and the iguana didn't protest. That surprised Mckenzie Garcia, who'd helped take care of Heineken. "He wouldn't let us get near him," Mckenzie said. The cats were given to Angel in carriers, and the dogs were walked out on leashes. Angel bent down and kissed them all as they jumped all over her. Before she left, workers gave her dog and cat food from a trailer filled with donations.

Angel loaded the food and her menagerie into her SUV, putting the pets who weren't in carriers on her children's laps, and then they happily drove away.

The remaining odd mix of pets not claimed by their owners, including dozens of fish, a squirrel, a hamster found in the middle of a deserted intersection, and a half dozen rabbits of different colors and types, were placed in foster care. Many of these animals were fostered by the Animal Ark rescue group in Minnesota and HOPE Safehouse in Wisconsin. Regardless of species, they, just like the cats and dogs, went into homes or were fostered.

14

Animal Mug Shots

ACH DAY FOR SEVERAL MONTHS, residents who had been evac-uated out of New Orleans drove from Texas, Louisiana, Arkansas, and Alabama to Camp Tylertown, hoping to find their pets. One at a time—in groups, and sometimes with as many as six members to a family—they filed into the tiny office. Sometimes it was so cramped that there was little room to move.

They quietly thumbed through the several hundred photos and admissions paperwork sandwiched inside a growing number of three-ring binders. When they found their pets, they'd exclaim, "I think I found my dog!" or, "Here's my kitty." Many were overcome with emotion. If their pets had been placed in temporary foster care, arrangements were made to reunite them at a later date.

One couple, Laneka Campbell and Reggie Williams, went to the center looking for Covoo, their Yorkshire Terrier, named after the lion in the film *Simba's Pride*.

They had lost their dog when Reggie, asleep with Covoo on the Causeway bridge (which runs across Lake Pontchartrain), was awakened in the middle of the night and an animal control offi-cer took Covoo from him. Laneka had left earlier with Reggie's father, but Reggie stayed with the dog until he was ordered to leave his home and was taken to the Causeway, a staging area where evacuees were told to wait for buses to transport them out of the flooded area. All Reggie had in his hand was a piece of paper with the name and address of a shelter. He thought he'd been given a receipt that he could match up with an ID tag on his dog, but that wasn't the case. After he was evacuated and able to return to the area, Reggie followed instructions and went to the animal shelter, but Covoo wasn't there. Workers suggested he try the Camp Tylertown rescue center.

Reggie and Laneka arrived at camp late one morning. They looked through the binders and found Covoo's paperwork and photo. Although they were happy to find Covoo, the disappointment showed on their faces when they learned he'd been placed in foster care and they wouldn't see him for another week or so, to allow time for transportation arrangements to be made. They were told that many of the animals were placed in temporary homes for their own safety, to prevent possible exposure to illnesses that might be carried in by pets still arriving from New Orleans, and also to make room for newly rescued arrivals.

The couple looked sad. Then Reggie asked if they could hold Mia, my foster Chihuahua who was in the small office with us, saying he needed a dog fix. I picked up eight-pound Mia from her bed, where she was napping under a table, and handed her to him. She's the kind of dog who loves to be held and will put her head on a shoulder. As Reggie held the little dog against his chest and Laneka petted her, the couple stood there in silence.

A week later, Covoo was driven back to base camp. Reggie and Laneka were notified and returned to pick him up. A big deal was made over the reunion, and this time Laneka and Reggie left base camp smiling with Covoo safely in tow.

The next day, another New Orleans man arrived at base camp looking for his dog, a Rottweiler. The man went from run to run and then looked through the binders, searching for his dog's photo. He didn't find him. That afternoon, however, he decided to try to get into his neighborhood. He went through an unmanned roadblock and made it into his area and then onto his rubble-strewn street. As he slowly drove through his neighborhood, an animal control officer driving a truck headed his way. He waved down the driver, who stopped. He got out of his car and showed the officer photos of his dog from his wallet, and then gave the officer his street address, which was up the road.

He could hardly believe what the animal control officer said next. "That's *your* dog? I picked him up a couple of days after the storm. He's been staying with me at the shelter." The man got back in his car and followed the officer to the facility, where he retrieved his dog. He wanted to share the good news, so he called the St. Francis Animal Sanctuary to let us know.

When people arrived at base camp looking for their pets, some wanted so badly for a dog or a cat to be theirs that they would point to one, then another, and yet another and say, "There he is," before realizing the pets weren't theirs. One woman walked with her husband through the Heights area at Camp Tylertown looking for their Rottweiler. "That's him!" the woman said.

"No, honey, look at the face," her husband told her. "That's not his face."

"This one is him," she said when they reached a second run where another male Rottweiler was housed.

"It's not him," her husband said quietly. They weren't able to find their dog, at least not at Camp Tylertown.

In a similar case, a woman arrived at base camp looking for her female Siamese kitten. She found one, but the kitten was much younger than the cat she was looking for. This one, barely eight weeks old, was born just before the storm. Plus—and this made the reunion unlikely—this kitten was rescued twenty miles from where the woman's kitty was left. "She swam twenty miles!" the woman told volunteers. No one had the heart to tell her a kitten that age could not have survived drifting twenty miles in storm waters. No inquiries had been made about the rescued kitten, so the woman filled out foster paperwork, even though she believed she had found her own lost kitty.

When pet owner John David found a photo in a lost-and-found binder of Sadie, his tan Chow, he returned to base camp a second time to make sure she wasn't in a run he'd overlooked. He was given contact information for the foster home in northern California where Sadie was staying. Then he got in his car and drove twenty-three hundred miles to the San Francisco Bay Area to pick her up. He didn't want to wait for transportation arrangements to be made. He couldn't take another day without Sadie. He wanted her home with his other two dogs.

John had not left Sadie behind. On August 29, he had taken the three-year-old dog to work with him in downtown New Orleans and left his other two dogs, Nicky and Andy, at his home just outside the French Quarter. When John left for an appointment in Gulfport, Sadie stayed with an employee at his Julia Street flower shop. Once John heard radio reports that the storm was looming, he tried to drive back to New Orleans, but police at roadblocks turned him away. He was not able to make it home near the French Quarter, either. He was forced to turn around. Then, a few days later, on CNN, he watched as a military officer jumped the fence to his home, "and there were my other two dogs. I knew they were okay." When he was allowed back in, he returned to his home and learned that neighbors had left food and water for his dogs. "It really restores my faith in people," he said. "It was amazing to me." There were signs that the two dogs had escaped the storm water by going into the house from the yard, where he'd left them, to the second floor. And that's where they stayed until the water receded. He also discovered that his dogs had gone through a case of vitamins. "These dogs literally chewed all my vitamin bottles open. You can't tell me dogs don't know what's good for them," he added. "They opened and ate them all."

Sadie, meanwhile, was still gone from the store. John was determined to get her back. When Sadie saw John for the first time after he arrived in northern California, "she came running up to me, put her paws on my shoulders and started licking my face," he said. "She is just a big ol' baby." She looked at him, he said, as if to say, "I've been sitting here waiting and saying, 'Where have you been?'" He put her in their car, and they drove back to Louisiana.

Sadie still goes to work with John each day. But now, even for out-of-state business trips, "I take her with me, and she doesn't leave my side. She has always been close to me. Since she's been back, we're even closer."

Sadie, John says, doesn't think she's a dog. "She's so much more. She's my friend. I just don't know what I'd do without her."

For pet owners like Laneka Campbell, Reggie Williams, and John David, finding their dogs in the Camp Tylertown binders—proof positive that they had been saved—was comforting. Those binders were their link to their pets, putting them one step closer to getting them back.

"I was so amazed when I looked in a book of photos, and there was Sadie," John said.

15

Reunions

For MANY OF THE VOLUNTEERS working with rescued animals, their mission was to reunite pets with their owners. In the case of Elana Gerson, a volunteer caregiver, a phone call made all the difference in one family's life. Elana was volunteering in the dog area at the Celebration Station triage center in January 2006 when she noticed that a yellow Lab's original ID tag was still on her collar. Elana used her cell phone to dial the number. Amy Kimball, Sadie's person, answered the phone.

Amy couldn't get to Sadie quickly enough. She and her sister-in-law, Karen, jumped in the car and drove to Celebration Station from St. Bernard Parish. It was normally a forty-five-minute drive, but Amy and Karen made it in twenty minutes. When they arrived, Amy told workers that Sadie had had an angel—her brother-in-law Walter—looking after her. It was nothing short of a miracle, she said, that brought Sadie back to them after more than four months of being apart.

The last time Amy had seen Sadie was on August 28, 2005, in the home she shared with her fiancé, Tommy Cosse, in St. Bernard Parish. They evacuated before the hurricane and believed they'd be back in a couple of days. Before leaving, they set out food and water for Sadie. But their neighborhood was one of the hardest hit, and they weren't allowed back in for several weeks. When residents were allowed to return home, Tommy drove to their house, hoping Sadie was still there and okay. When he found the remains of a dog in the side yard, he reported to Amy that Sadie hadn't made it. After all, for fifteen days, the parish had been flooded with standing water; it would have been difficult for Sadie to survive.

Tommy's brother Walter, however, wasn't convinced that it was Sadie who had perished on the side of their house. He insisted to his wife, Karen, that Sadie was a swimmer and could have saved herself. He knew firsthand, because he and Tommy had often taken Sadie fishing. She was an experienced swimmer. Someone had to have her, he told Karen. Walter returned to his brother's house to see for himself, and he found pawprints on the roof. They had to be Sadie's, he told anyone who would listen. She was alive, and he was determined to find her. He made fliers, hung them in the neighborhood, and posted listings online with Sadie's information.

Before he learned Sadie's fate, however, Walter was killed in a construction accident. He was working in a hurricane-damaged area, helping residents rebuild their homes.

About two months later, while the family was still grieving, Amy answered her phone. Elana Gerson was calling to tell her that Sadie was safe and at Celebration Station.

Karen was convinced that it was her late husband Walter who'd helped Sadie find her way home. To Elana, who'd made that important phone call, "If that's not a miracle, I don't know what is."

Reunions such as this one felt like miracles, given all that the owners and pets had been through. To see them together again was what the animal rescue effort was all about.

"Reunion! Reunion!" rang out across the grounds at Camp Tylertown and, later, Celebration Station each time a pet went home. The banging together of pots and pans—and later the ringing of a cowbell—could be heard across the grounds, letting everyone know that another hurricane victim had been reunited with a pet. For the caregivers who couldn't leave their posts, it made their day to hear that sound. Reunions were the events volunteers and staffers looked forward to most.

For the pets' families, they meant even more. Every owner had a story about how they came to lose their pets. Volunteers listened intently as owners arrived, day after day, in search of their pets and retold what they'd been through.

Lee and Sheila Glazier told one such story on September 25, after they drove onto the sanctuary grounds knowing that Diago, their buff-colored Cocker Spaniel, was there. Diago was wearing a rabies tag that had been traced back to the Glaziers. Sheila and Lee had gotten onto the Petfinder Web site, where Diago's photo and rabies tag information were posted. From that tag, a positive match was made. The next day they drove from Georgia, where they had been evacuated, to Tylertown's base camp, hoping that their three other dogs might have been saved, too. After they arrived, they walked to Toytown to the small dogs. But only Diago was there. Not finding their other three didn't dampen their enthusiasm for reuniting with Diago, however. When Diago and the Glaziers saw one another, it was difficult to tell who was happier. Diago's entire body wagged as he saw his owners for the first time since the storm. He went from one to the other, jumping up. For the Glaziers, getting Diago was good enough, they said. To find even one was a relief.

Witnessing a reunion was also good enough for volunteer Barb Davis, a Nebraskan who spent two months in the Gulf region. She volunteered at the Celebration Station triage center. "We came in one night from tracking and trapping. It was close to midnight, and a dog and a cat were being reunited with two different families. That was the only time these people could get there, at midnight.

"It made me want to go out and find more so we could get even more pets reunited with their families. We worked twenty-hour days, and the hope of a reunion was the driving force. It lifted morale." Buoyed by good feelings from reunions, volunteers started the next day anew, refreshed to find more lost animals.

The reunion process was an integral part of the rescue operation. In the aftermath of the storm, the process at Camp
Tylertown began in earnest almost from the moment the base
camp was set up. Reunions even became my second job. My first
day at camp, I responded to requests from the command center
to see if I could physically match up pets from information given
by owners to the command center. That first day, I made two
matches. The first was Brooklyn, a small red Pomeranian, who
was delivered a few weeks later to her foster mom. The second
was Kika, a Schnauzer. Lost-and-found workers immediately notified Kika's person, Mike Pyle, who said, upon seeing Kika the following day, that he had never expected to see his dog again. As
more people learned of the rescue center and called the St.
Francis Animal Sanctuary or the Best Friends command center in
Utah, reunions snowballed.

One of the best ways to make those reunions happen was the
daily posting on the Petfinder Web site of each animal who
arrived at base camp. Volunteers did most of the data input, a job
that had the perk of being indoors, so they could escape from the
heat of the day. It was through Petfinder that Claudia and Ernest
Seymour found their eleven-year-old dog, Jaque.

They logged on to Petfinder from Houston, where they'd
moved, looking for the dog they hadn't seen in nearly a month.
He was taken away from them on the Causeway bridge at
Interstate 10. They searched through the hundreds of listings of
dogs, one by one. Then they saw him. A photo of their Lhasa
Apso mix was posted on Petfinder with a notation that his last
known location was in Mississippi at Camp Tylertown. On
October 1, the Seymours drove from Houston to Camp
Tylertown to retrieve him and have their reunion.

Other evacuees, ones who found their animals on Petfinder
or traveled to base camp to look for them, were also successful.
Gizmo, a Jack Russell mix, went home to owners Theresa and

Henry Schloner. Skiddles, a tabby cat who resembled a skunk, was reunited with his person, Pat Murphy, as was Princess, a Siamese cat, who went home to Cheryl Bradley. A Chow mix named Shorty, a Pit Bull named Sable, and a Siberian Husky called Brie also were returned to their families. They, among hundreds of others, got to go home. For the ones who weren't reunited, volunteers and animal humane groups from around the country were in the wings, waiting with open arms to give them new homes.

Originally, no grand plan was in place at base camp because the response to Katrina had been so immediate. Before long, procedures were improvised and processes fell into place, especially as a result of Petfinder's large database of animals and the volunteers who worked tirelessly to make matches. By September 19, twenty-six dogs and cats had been returned to their people. By the end of October, two hundred had been reunited. When the last reunion took place in December 2006, around 15 percent of the pets rescued by Best Friends had been reunited.

It wasn't an easy job, matching people and pets. After victims were evacuated from New Orleans, they began sending pleas via e-mails and photos, hoping for help finding their pets. Those descriptions were passed on to base camp, where volunteers looked for the animals in dog runs and cat kennels, hoping to make a match. But Camp Tylertown wasn't the only place animals were taken to. They were also at the handful of other temporary animal shelters in the area; and rescue groups from other states went into the area, rescued dogs and cats from the streets, and took them out of state. As one volunteer at base camp described it, pets were scattered to the four winds. But the workers at Camp Tylertown did their best to make sure each animal picked up was put in the database and listed on Petfinder before he or she went to a foster home.

Pets with rabies tags or microchips were simpler to match, although it became frustrating when phone numbers didn't work; it took months to get cell phone towers and land-line cables repaired and service restored. As telephone service slowly returned to the city, volunteers redialed the numbers, hoping to reach owners, as in the case of Sadie the yellow Lab. But even then, phone service was poor at best, and it wasn't uncommon for calls to be dropped several times. (It was no joke when staffers and volunteers, moving a foot or two on the lawn for a better connection, could be heard saying, "Can you hear me now?")

For the Pomeranian named Brooklyn, after initial contact with her owner was made, the number died and went out of service. No one had Brooklyn's person's address.

The Pomeranian was placed in a foster home in the town where her owner had relocated in hopes that her owner would contact the lost-and-found workers again. Information was put on the Internet, and the foster guardian contacted the media to get the word out that Brooklyn was in the city and waiting to be picked up. The ploy worked, and Brooklyn was reunited.

Some animals were matched by chance, and many volunteers, like Elana Gerson, were the heroes. One day in September, a volunteer, during her second trip to Camp Tylertown, was sitting in the small office waiting for the paperwork to be completed for two more foster dogs when she looked up at the dozens of photos of lost pets tacked to the wall. All of a sudden, she blurted out, "Oh, my gosh, I think that's my foster boy." The photo was blurry and the dog had since been groomed, but the volunteer was certain it was him. She called a friend, who agreed to go to her home where her boyfriend was watching her pets and drive the dog back to Tylertown, where his person picked up the dog.

Another early reunion was that of Buddy, a brown-marble-colored American Staffordshire Terrier (a relative of the Pit Bull). When she couldn't locate Buddy after the storm, Buddy's person, Heather Taylor, sent out two hundred e-mails and fliers with Buddy's photo to both human and pet rescue groups, the Red Cross, veterinarians, and even pet stores, hoping someone had seen him. She searched feverishly for any word about Buddy, who is her son Allen's dog. She never gave up hope. "When you have lost everything you own," she said, "and have little money and means, it is hard. We lost our home, possessions, our car, just like many other people." Still, she persevered. "This is Heather Taylor and I am one of thousands of people searching for their pets," her e-mails began.

An e-mail from Heather was received at the command center. Heather's description of Buddy said that he is "a big friendly baby who responds well to his name." At that point, we didn't yet have a printer set up at base camp, so I enlarged the photo of Buddy on my laptop's monitor and walked outside, with the computer in hand, to Pooch Alley (where most of the Pit Bulls were housed) to see whether I could match a dog to Buddy's photo. Running Pit Alley that day was volunteer John Hoenemeier. I showed John the fuzzy photo, and together we walked from run to run, searching for a look-alike. We came upon a dark-brown brindled boy. One of the problems was that this dog's face was cut up and the one in the photo wasn't. And we weren't quite sure about the markings. The description was explicit about the shape of the white fur on his chest, but because of the angle of the camera, we weren't positive. This dog's run had been moved about five feet away from the next one on the row because he was possessive and he and his neighbor would get into it through the chain link, giving the dog surface cuts and scrapes. Yet John and I were 90 percent sure the dog was Buddy.

I took photos of the dog, went back to the office, and e-mailed a note and photos to Jill Dennis at the command center's lost-and-found office, letting her know that we had a dog at Camp Tylertown who looked a lot like Buddy. Because there was a strong possibility it was Buddy, we sent him to Texas with a volunteer.

In the meantime, Heather enlisted help from another rescue group, who went to her house to look for Buddy, but he wasn't there either. Heather didn't know about Camp Tylertown and wasn't aware that Buddy had been safely removed from the house while the water was still standing in the parish. That rescue had happened on September 11, when volunteers Tracey Simmons from Chicago and Ken Ray of Pell City, Alabama, were out in a flat-bottomed jon boat and headed to Paulger Street after they heard a dog barking. A dark-brown Pit Bull was making his way down the street by jumping up on a porch, then back down into the water, and back up onto another porch. He caught Tracey and Ken's attention, and they motored down the street. They heard a second dog bark from inside one of the houses. They opened the front door, and Buddy waded in the water toward them.

"Buddy was happy to see humans," Tracey said. "He was ready to be rescued. It was like he was relieved. He didn't mind the boat ride at all." But Buddy had to share the boat with the Pit Bull and a cat who were rescued from the same street. "Buddy wanted to go after the Pit," she said. "That was his only problem. Buddy was very much a people dog, just not a dog-friendly type of dog." The other dog was trying to jump out of the boat, so Tracey pinned him with her knees while Ken kept Buddy up front with him to prevent any scuffles.

Heather's then six-year-old son Allen was despondent over losing Buddy. Heather and her two children had been living in San Antonio when the hurricane hit, but Allen was visiting his father in New Orleans at the time. Allen and Buddy were insepa-rable, so much so that when Allen went to his dad's for summer vacation, Buddy went with him. Allen's father, thinking they would be gone only a couple of days, left Buddy inside the house with food and water, not knowing that storm water on some streets in his neighborhood would reach the ceiling. Somehow, Buddy survived by treading water until it dropped to where he could sit on the sofa.

Just when she was ready to give up on finding Buddy, Heather got a call from the Best Friends rescue center, saying they'd received her e-mails and photos and wanted her to look at some photos of a dog at base camp who looked like Buddy.

"They e-mailed me photos of the dog they thought was Buddy, and I almost fell out of my chair," Heather said. She was certain it was he. If not, she said, she'd adopt the look-alike.

In late September 2005, Allen and Buddy were reunited near Houston. Allen looked at Buddy and said, "I thought the hurricane washed you away." A year later, instead of vacationing in New Orleans again, Allen spent it at home in Texas with Buddy, playing ball and swimming together in their pool. "They're still inseparable," Heather said. She was so grateful to have Buddy back that she broke a rule after he returned home: she now lets him sit wherever he likes, including on the furniture.

Many animals, especially the small ones, were moved to foster homes to get them into temporary housing until their families could be found. One day at base camp, I walked over to Toytown looking for a black Poodle named Tia, because the command center was making arrangements to get her back to her person. A match had just been made, however, so Tia had inadvertently been sent with a San Francisco Bay Area group and was, at that moment, in the air on her way to California and about to be placed in a foster home. It took several phone calls by a couple of people to hook up with the folks awaiting the flight in California. They were asked to hold the Poodle at their facility until arrangements could be made to transport her back to her person, who had evacuated to Texas. That was done, and Tia was flown to Texas and reunited with her person on November 1.

Jill and Steve Williams, foster parents to a puppy terrier they named Yoda, flew with him at their expense to his Louisiana home in time for Christmas. They wanted him to be home, but giving him up was bittersweet. "When we got the news that Yoda's family had been located, he had already been staying with us for a few months," Jill said. "It may not seem like a long time in retrospect, but when we first started fostering him, he was just a tiny, lonely, whimpering pup. He was only three or four months old at the time, so he was confused and sick and scared. We watched him quickly grow into a fearless, happy, and—most importantly—healthy dog."

When she got the call that Yoda's family was looking for "Boss," his original name, a feeling of panic came over Jill. "I had so many questions: Was this really his family? Would he remember them? Would he be sad to leave us? My tears were quickly brushed aside when I mustered the courage to phone [his family] and talk to them. They were beyond happy to hear from me, and repeatedly thanked us while crying and talking about Boss."

Their lives, Jill said, had been turned upside down by the storm. "This was the first bright point in weeks for them. It was almost Christmas, and I knew that this would mean the world to them—to have their pup back in time for the holidays. I wanted to be a part of that joy. I wanted to see the smiles on their faces." Seeing Yoda go home was also a way to bring about closure for Jill's family. So they flew to New Orleans on December 15. Because Yoda had been such a young puppy, he was shy at first in his original home. But when his housemate, Smokey, a Pomeranian, was returned a short time later, the two immediately remembered each other and haven't stopped playing since. "This was the best present anyone could ever get," Jill said.

Not all foster parents, however, willingly gave up the dogs and cats they'd taken in after Hurricane Katrina when the owners surfaced to reclaim them. The prospect of giving up the animals they helped and came to love was a difficult one, and a small percentage of those who took in fosters from Camp Tylertown refused. As a result, in an attempt to get their pets back, roughly twenty Katrina survivors sued humane societies, animal rescue groups, and people who had taken in animals.

With Best Friends, it was just the opposite. The organization stood by the pets and the original guardians and was the plaintiff in lawsuits, in concert with the Louisiana Attorney General's office, on behalf of the legal and rightful pet owners. In Louisiana, pets are still considered pieces of property. To that end, Best Friends followed the letter of the law.

One of those cases was one of the last reunions facilitated by Best Friends. The suit involved a small dog, a Shih Tzu mix named Little Bit by volunteers. The circumstances surrounding Little Bit being taken from his family were similar to the story of Snowball, a small, fluffy dog removed from the arms of a child by a police officer. No one was ever able to find Snowball or his owners. In fact, the circumstances were almost identical, except for the location. The Associated Press reported that Snowball had been taken away from a crying boy at the Superdome, whereas Little Bit was taken from a crying toddler on the Causeway, about five miles away.

Little Bit's family punched a hole through the roof of their flooded Mereaux home in St. Bernard Parish and lifted their pets out with them. "We took three dogs and two birds through the roof of our house," owner Lisa Downs said. They had to leave their cats behind.

A rescuer in a boat allowed the dogs and birds to go with them, but once they arrived at Interstate 10 near the Causeway, they were told by uniformed officers to leave their pets. Lisa and her boyfriend, Robert Carter, tied their two larger dogs, Jordan and Cee-Cee, to a fence on the other side of the river. Jordan, thirteen years old, was too weak to walk, and they had to carry him to the fence. They released the birds.

The family kept Little Bit with them as they stood in line waiting to board the bus with Lisa's young son, Devin. "I had my son in one arm and Little Bit in the other," Lisa said. "The bus driver said, 'You're not bringing that dirty dog on this bus.'"

He told Lisa to let the dog go. Her son pleaded with him to let them keep him. "He cried and said, 'No, don't let him go,'" Lisa said. But the driver refused, so Robert walked Little Bit to a nearby field and let him loose.

Little Bit was ultimately rescued and taken to Best Friends' Camp Tylertown site and eventually placed in foster care. A neighbor looked for the family's other two dogs and was told they hadn't made it.

Micci Childers, a worker with Stealth Volunteers—a group that helps people find their pets by combing through hundreds of photos and e-mails to match up identifying information—assisted Lisa in locating Little Bit.

Later, when Lisa's family returned to their neighborhood to see what they could find, "I spotted one of my cats," Lisa said. "He survived by hanging around the neighborhood. The other one, Midnight, a neighbor found and took care of."

Because the home Little Bit was placed in didn't want to give her up, Best Friends filed a lawsuit in the county where the dog was placed. Due to that move, Little Bit was reunited with her person fifteen months after the storm, also just in time for the holidays.

"I always knew I would see him again," said Lisa, who started looking for her missing dog almost as soon as she and her family were evacuated. "It's like a 150-pound weight has been lifted off my back." Once home again, Little Bit wouldn't let Lisa out of his sight. "He follows me everywhere," she said. "He sleeps with me. When he first saw me, he squirmed away from the person who was holding him to get to me, he was so excited." She said he's back to normal, wrestling and playing with her son. "It's such a joy to see them back together and a joy to have at least one of my babies back. It does give us that closure we needed."

For one East New Orleans woman, getting just one of her dogs back—and knowing that the other was placed in a good home—was good enough for her.

Jackie Jones stayed for two weeks in Orleans Parish near City Park after Katrina hit because she didn't want to leave her dogs. She had rescued Blackie and Angel two years earlier as starving strays under an overpass in the Ninth Ward, where they had been fending for themselves. She took them home, fattened them up, and had them spayed. She also put them on heartworm prevention. "I stayed because of them," Jackie said. "I kept thinking, 'The water will go down.' I had about forty gallons of water and bags and bags of dog food. I had keys to my neighbor's house, and she had canned goods and water. So we stayed on a neighbor's porch." But then the water did not go down. "People in boats offered rides," she continued. "I gave a man a couple dollars to boat us to a service station. We left the neighbor's porch, and the two dogs and I stayed at the service station for a week. The National Guard came and said we had to leave because we were on private property. They came back a day later and told me it was mandatory, I had one day to leave, and I couldn't take my dogs. I told them if my dogs drown, I drown, too, because that's why I stayed. Two weeks after the storm, I had to leave my dogs upstairs at my neighbor's house." She left enough food to last two weeks and enough water for five days. She paid the man again for a ride in a boat and was taken to St. Charles Avenue in Carrolton, to a National Guard staging area. The Guard then took her to the Convention Center and, after two days, to the airport in Kenner. She was bused to Alton, Illinois, where she stayed for about six months.

When Jackie returned to New Orleans, she read a newspaper ad about a Best Friends adoption event at Celebration Station in Metairie and later learned while there that her dogs had been rescued and were okay. She also found out that Blackie had been picked up from her neighbor's porch five days after Jackie evacuated. "She was waiting for me," Jackie said. "That touched me. She's a good girl. I missed her." A volunteer has helped her find both her dogs in a database. Blackie, who was called Olive by volunteers, was reunited with Jackie two weeks later. Her other dog, Angel, was adopted out, and that was fine with Jackie. "Because I know she's in a home with a family and she's okay, I'm happy. I got Blackie back, and she's doing fine. They took care of her the way I did." Jackie has since relocated to Baton Rouge, where she and Blackie are living with family. "We're happy here," Jackie said.

The same weekend Blackie was reunited with Jackie, Leah Purcell, with Spindletop Refuge in Houston, returned an aging Pit Bull named Old Girl to her person. Old Girl had been picked up as a stray by an independent rescuer a month after the storm and taken to Camp Tylertown, where she was treated for a wound in her mouth and an infected eye. In November, Leah fostered Old Girl and drove to her shelter in Texas.

Leah was creative when it came to matching people with their pets. Out of the approximately 400 Pit Bulls and mixes she took out of New Orleans—210 of which were from Best Friends—she reunited more than 25 percent of them, including 40 from Camp Tylertown and Celebration Station. One day, after driving Old Girl to Orleans Parish near City Park to her original owner, Leah and a friend stopped to talk to a resident in a neighborhood where only a few people had returned. Leah had mailed notices to residents and left postcards at their doors, informing them that their dogs were safe. She was looking for an owner on that street because she didn't have the house number. "We were on the street and saw a man in a truck," Leah said. "We stopped him to ask if he knew some people who lived in the neighborhood who had a Pit Bull. He said, 'My two dogs are still missing.' He had photos in his car. I looked at the photos and said, 'I have your dogs!'" Leah returned the dogs to him a few weeks later on her next trip to New Orleans.

Leah also helped locate owners for Dr. Karen Dashfield, a veterinarian who had put her Newton, New Jersey, veterinary practice on hold to foster Katrina dogs. Leah had gotten a team of volunteers together and had gone door to door putting postcards on houses in neighborhoods where specific dogs were found, letting residents know where the dogs were. So Leah did the same for many of the dogs Karen was fostering. Missy, a temperamental older Chow whose elderly owners had health problems and couldn't take her back, stayed with Karen for nearly two years until Missy was placed with an animal trainer. "She'll live the rest of her life with her," Karen said.

Another rescue group, Out of the Pitts in Kingston, in upstate New York, was so picky about who their American Pit Bull Terriers went to—and was still hoping to reunite them with their original owners—that Rose Norkus, a volunteer with the group, didn't place the final dogs until two years after Katrina. One was Danielle, a dog Rose described as weighing just thirty-five or forty pounds but "tough as nails."

"She's great with human beings," but not so good with other dogs. She stayed in a foster home until that perfect single-dog home came along. It happened in the fall of 2007 when Danielle went to live with an environmental scientist and her husband near the animal rescue in upstate New York. "They have an all-natural environment and habitat in their backyard," Rose said. "There's a little stream and trees, and Danielle thinks when she's back there that she's in the woods. It's a perfect home. They found a restaurant where they can take her out to dinner with them."

Out of the Pitts also reunited a couple of the dogs long after they'd fostered them. One was a Pit Bull mix called Bonnie at Camp Tylertown, although her real name turned out to be Pepper. The owners of Bonnie wanted her back immediately, but Rose was hesitant. That's because the owner had arranged for his brother, who lived in New Orleans, to take his dog to a fenced vacant lot, leave her there, and visit daily to give her food and water. "I told him I wasn't withholding his dog," Rose said, "but when he was in a situation where she could live with him, we'd return her." Seven months later, the owner and his two young sons drove to New York from Virginia, where they'd relocated, to pick up Pepper. "She knew him," Rose said. The two boys, then about eight and thirteen, cried when they saw Pepper for the first time. "It was a big deal," Rose said. "The media was here to cover it."

Then, in November 2006, a pet medical center in Virginia informed the group that a car had hit Pepper and her leg needed to be amputated. Without the surgery, she'd have to be put down. The owner told Rose that Pepper had been playing outside with his youngest son when she ran into the street and got hit.

"[The owner] said he couldn't afford the surgery, and he would give her back to me if only we'd save her life," Rose said. "That said a lot. He didn't need to give her back to us." Out of the Pitts paid the $2,100 surgical cost, and Pepper survived.

Since then, Rose has received regular photos of Pepper playing, now with three legs, in the house with her family. "Everybody's happy," Rose said. "It's clear they love her."

Some owners were confident they'd find their pets, even though it sometimes took a while. Such was the case with a tortoiseshell cat named Lightning. When Robert Rodriguez and his family located Lightning at Camp Tylertown, he said they had never doubted they'd get her back. She was smart, he said, and that worked in her favor. They had tried to evacuate with her, but they couldn't find her and had to leave quickly. Still, he said, he knew she'd be okay. And when they walked up to her kennel at base camp and called her name, she started meowing.

For volunteers at base camp, reunions like Lightning's inspired them to keep going. On the morning of September 12, a special moment took place when New Orleans resident Gallee Grimshaw arrived looking for his cat, ATaonTaCaun. On September 2, Gallee had left his five-year-old cat with Jefferson Parish Animal Control.

A couple of days later, he set out to find ATaonTaCaun. He went from shelter to shelter, but no one could tell him where his cat was. His last hope was when a shelter worker told him about the Best Friends relief center. Gallee got in a rental car and headed for St. Francis. Once there, he walked into the cattery, and it took less than a minute for him to find his cat. He picked ATaonTaCaun up and cried as the cat leaned his head against Gallee's shoulder. Then, for the first time that day, pots and pans were clanked together and the cry "Reunion! Reunion!" belted out from a bullhorn, alerting workers on the grounds that a cat was being reunited with his person.

When asked afterward where he was headed, Gallee, a model, said he had no place to go because of the flooding in his city. Then he said he wanted to help and asked if he could stay on at Camp Tylertown to volunteer. "Absolutely," he was told. Because

Gallee was trained at handling Rottweilers, Sherry Woodard enlisted his help at Pit Alley, caring for the Pit Bulls, Mastiffs, Great Danes, Rotties, and other large dogs housed there.

When a couple arrived at the Tylertown base camp one night to retrieve BayBay, an English Cocker Spaniel who had survived nearly a month in a backyard storage shed, the reunion lifted everyone's spirits. BayBay was reunited with Connie and Dwight Fitch of Gentilly a week after her rescue.

The triage center was full, so BayBay, along with a handful of other dogs, had recuperated in a large kennel in the office at Tylertown. When I didn't go into the field or wasn't walking the grounds at the rescue center looking for matches of cats and dogs from e-mails and photos, that office was where I wrote at my laptop. It's also where I slept each night, in a sleeping bag on the floor, after spending the first week sleeping on the porch and in the laundry room. Because of that, I was with BayBay just about twenty-four hours a day the week after her rescue. She was one sick girl.

Before evacuating, Dwight Fitch had stacked concrete blocks and wood to make a staircase from the ground to the ceiling of the shed in case the area flooded. He put dog food on the steps for BayBay. Then he and his wife, Connie, evacuated. "I still don't know how she survived in that storage shed," Connie said. "It had at least five feet of water in it."

When BayBay was rescued from the shed, a local police officer on the street, who knew the Fitches, handed her over to Cliff Deutsch, a sergeant at the time with a Florida sheriff's department who was out rescuing that day. The local officer also gave Cliff the Fitches' cell phone number. The Fitches were called as soon as BayBay was driven to base camp. Seven days later, the Fitches drove in from Arkansas, where they'd evacuated to.

When Connie called BayBay's name at Camp Tylertown, it didn't appear that BayBay knew who was calling her. She sniffed the ground and didn't look up. "BayBay!" Connie said a bit louder. With that, BayBay lifted her head and walked over to Connie, staring at her and sniffing the air. "BayBay, it's me," Connie said.

Then suddenly, BayBay's entire body wagged, and she recognized her person. She threw herself against Connie, who had knelt down, and licked her face. Volunteers and staffers stood there watching. Instead of sadness, everyone was beaming. One more pet was going home to her people.

Back home, BayBay is still wagging her tail. "She's so happy now," Connie said. Before Katrina, BayBay had spent a lot of time outside. Now she spends her days and nights in the house. "At night, BayBay likes to sleep underneath the dining room table," Connie said. "There's a tablecloth, and it's like a tent. She goes under there, and she's out like a light." But she has spunk, too. "She's six years old, but she has a lot of energy," Connie said. "She loves her walks. I've been taking her on walks at night because it's so hot right now during the day. She can't wait to get inside."

A cat named Garfield was reunited several weeks after the storm, but almost by accident. The Tyson family e-mailed photos back and forth with Rude Ranch animal rescue in Haywood, Maryland. One in particular looked like their feline. The resemblance was close enough that Nita Tyson and her twelve-year-old daughter made the two-hour drive from Front Royal, Virginia, to see for themselves. They were disappointed when they arrived and realized he wasn't Garfield after all. While there, however, Bob Rude, who runs the rescue with his wife, showed Nita some other cats, even though he thought it was a longshot that any of them was Garfield. Nita stopped at one kennel to take a closer look, and there was Garfield. The Rudes called him Bite Boy.

"He arrived at Camp Tylertown with a lot of bite wounds on the lower half of his body, and he had a nasty upper respiratory infection," Bob said. "He was never all that friendly with people and would only tolerate us." But when they got him out of his kennel, he rolled over and "started pawing the air and showing definite signs of recognition," Bob said. Before Nita and her daughter left for home with Garfield, Nita called her husband to let him know that she had seen a stray neighborhood cat called Itsy Bitsy hanging around near the rescue. Nita wanted to adopt the stray, so the family returned a few weeks later to take Itsy Bitsy home, too.

For many pets, it was as if they'd resigned themselves to never finding their families. You could see it in their eyes, the deep sadness that had washed over them as the floodwater covered the streets and overtook their homes, leaving them stranded. That phase of their lives, in a home with people, seemed like a long-ago memory because so much had happened to them in between. When they were reunited, it seemed to come as a surprise. Volunteers who watched the reunions didn't take their eyes off the dogs and cats: the pets' looks were indifferent at first, but when they realized they were being called by their guardians, unforgettable signs of recognition filled their eyes.

A reunion of a different sort took place in January 2006 at Celebration Station's triage center between newborn puppies and their mother, a Miniature Pinscher mix. Her rescuer, Brenda, had dropped off the dog at the triage center the day before, because she, her husband, and their two young children were living in their car and couldn't care for the dog any longer. They'd found the dog, whom they'd named Pretty Mama, in late November, three months after the storm, in the backcountry eating from a pile of trash. Brenda and her husband took Pretty Mama in, not realizing she was pregnant. When Pretty Mama arrived, it was obvious to volunteers at Celebration Station that the dog was producing milk and had recently nursed pups. Brenda was asked where the babies were, and she said they had all found new homes.

Still, it didn't make sense that Pretty Mama's puppies could be old enough to be adopted out considering their mother was full of milk and obviously uncomfortable. For the next day and a half, Pretty Mama was inconsolable. When she was taken for walks, she desperately looked under every bush and around every corner, hoping to find her pups.

"She's frantic, looking about for her puppies," said Juliette Watt, a volunteer coordinator at the center. "It's heartbreaking. Isn't there anything we can do to ease her stress?" It appeared that

Pretty Mama was both distressed over being away from her puppies and in discomfort because she was engorged with milk.

Because Pretty Mama was so distraught, we called Brenda, who'd given us her number, to see if we could find out when the puppies were born and where they were. Brenda said all the adoptions had fallen through when the potential owners saw how young the puppies were. The babies, whose eyes were still closed, hadn't eaten, she said, since they'd been taken away from their mother.

"What should we do?" Brenda asked. "They're only three and a half weeks old."

"Bring them here so they can nurse," she was told.

A little later, around ten o'clock, Brenda walked into Celebration Station carrying a laundry basket. Inside were two female and two male puppies—two black, one red, and one tan—piled on top of one another. At first, it didn't look like they were breathing, but as we picked them up, they awakened and started whimpering.

What happened next was a relief to everyone at the center, especially Pretty Mama. As a group of volunteers stood to the side watching, the puppies were handed to the mama dog one by one. They immediately started to nurse while she was still on her feet. When her puppies were finished, Pretty Mama finally began to relax with her babies sound asleep against her belly. Brenda and her family left the center loaded with shampoo, soaps, toothpaste, handwipes, canned goods, and a children's book and stuffed animals for the kids—all donated items shipped to the center. Several volunteers and staffers took up a collection, and the family was given a handful of cash.

Pretty Mama, who that night was set up in a puppy room with her babies, lovingly nursed and cleaned up after them. She wasn't given a chance to be a mom, good or bad, when she was separated from her pups by people. A few days later, mama and babies left for a foster home. Brenda and her family's lives improved as well. Within a week they were living in a hotel in Metairie in government-subsidized temporary housing.

By being taken away from their mother so soon, the puppies were put at risk, said Kristi Littrell, a Best Friends adoption coordinator who has experience bottle-feeding newborns. "Eight weeks is a minimum age," she explained. "Usually, at six weeks they're weaned on gruel, but mom is still with them." In addition, she said, their immune systems are compromised without puppy milk. "If they're ripped away from mom, the puppy milk replacement doesn't have immunity boosters. Brenda helped save the puppies by taking them back to their mom."

16

A Dog Named Angel

A PIT BULL NAMED ANGEL, rescued from St. Bernard High School eighteen days after the storm, survived more than a hurricane. She was plucked from the second floor of the school, which had been the scene of a bloodbath against pets. Even so, pregnant Angel, along with Mercedes, Novocain, Daisy, and a handful of other dogs and cats, survived and was ultimately reunited with her family. The shootings at the school were an unfortunate—yet perhaps intentional, at the hands of rogue cops—side effect of the flooding of this Gulf Coast fishing community.

It all started when the entire parish of St. Bernard, much of which runs along the cypress-lined St. Bernard Highway, was underwater. The community was closer to the path of the storm than any other and was exposed to a surge of water from the Gulf of Mexico. It flooded in large part because of extensive levee failures along the Mississippi River Gulf Outlet Canal, a seventy-six-mile shipping channel.

Hundreds of evacuees in St. Bernard escaped the storm on August 29 by boating to three area schools (Sebastian Roy Elementary School, Beauregard Middle School, and St. Bernard High School), and many of them brought along their pets. A few days later, sheriff's deputies ordered them to get into the back of dump trucks—without their pets—so they could be dropped off at the nearby town of Violet. There, they would catch a barge to higher ground. The evacuees left, thinking that law enforcement officers would care for their pets. They were wrong.

Twenty-one-year-old Christopher Acosta was one of the residents who borrowed a boat to rescue friends and relatives—and their animals. Before the storm hit, Christopher sent his wife, who was in her ninth month of pregnancy, out of New Orleans to stay with family. He remained at their house with his dogs, Mercedes and Novocain, to try to ride out the storm. After the wall of water hit their house, he left with a few friends and family members and their dogs—twelve people in all. They got into his uncle's boat and motored to Beauregard Middle School in St. Bernard Parish. It took three trips, Christopher said, to get all their dogs to the school.

They stayed at the school for three days before sheriff's deputies ordered everyone to go. They had to leave their dogs, whom they were told would be cared for at an animal shelter. So the group left all the dogs except for Novocain. Christopher thought he'd be allowed to take one dog with him on the ferry, and since he convinced the deputies, Novocain went with him.

The group rode in a dump truck with other evacuees to the Violet boat launch. When Christopher was turned away because he had Novocain with him, he waded with his dog to the nearby levee in Violet, across St. Bernard Highway, and walked him to the top of the berm, where it was dry. He left Novocain on the levee and then made his way back to the boat launch to catch the last ferry out. Meanwhile, Mercedes was back at Beauregard Middle School, along with dogs belonging to Christopher's mother, uncle, cousin, and best friend.

After the refugees had been trucked from the schools to the Violet boat launch at Paris Road, they were ferried across the wide ribbon of the Mississippi River to the Algiers Landing on the west bank, at the foot of Canal Street overlooking the French Quarter. As they stepped off the barge, one of the first buildings they saw was the Algiers Courthouse. But justice was not meted out that day. It would, however, happen later.

Instead, parish residents were devastated to find out that the pets they'd entrusted to law enforcement officers had been killed.

Some learned that awful truth a few weeks later when CNN's Anderson Cooper, in early November 2005, broke the story that pets left at Beauregard Middle School had been shot to death. Retrieved from the scene were spent shells with the word "Tactical" imprinted on them, similar to police-issue munitions.

As soon as authorities gave the green light for residents to return home to St. Bernard Parish, a little more than two weeks later, Christopher Acosta drove straight to Beauregard Middle School where he'd left Mercedes. What he found were dead bodies, and that made him angry. The more bodies he saw, the angrier he got. He entered every classroom, searching. By his count, about forty deceased pets were in the building, including his mother's small Pomeranian. But Mercedes wasn't where he had left her. What Christopher didn't know at the time was that Mercedes was still at the school, alive but trapped.

More than a month later, on October 27, Maxey Nunez, a resident who lived nearby and had weathered the storm at his house, was at the school when he heard a faint whimper. He had gone to the school to turn off the water there in order to increase the pressure at his house. He stopped what he was doing and followed the sound to the gymnasium weight room behind the main school building. Just then, Maxey heard a car on the abandoned road and ran out to flag it down for help. The words "Animal Rescue" were scrawled on the car's side window, and inside were Kelle Davis, Samantha Holmes, and Barbara Dunsmore from Animal Rescue New Orleans. They parked the car, walked to the building with him, and found the whimpering dog, whose leash was stuck under a file cabinet. It was Mercedes. The three took her to Camp Tylertown's M*A*S*H Unit so she could be treated by a vet—who said she wouldn't have lasted much longer without water. Kelle later fostered Mercedes in her Texas home. In early January, with a CNN camera crew and a local newspaper reporter present, Mercedes was reunited outside the middle school with Christopher and his family, three months after they evacuated.

But most of the dogs weren't so lucky. Many were found dead, some tethered, others shot in groups and scattered in classrooms.

In two separate lengthy criminal probes—first looking into street shootings recorded by a photojournalist on the scene, and then into the firing upon pets at the three schools—the Louisiana attorney general's office in Baton Rouge sought justice. The findings of the investigators led straight to St. Bernard Parish sheriff's deputies, many of whom were entrusted with the care of nearly three hundred dogs, some cats, and a few birds left at the schools.

Photographer David Leeson, working for the *Dallas Morning News*, had been on assignment in New Orleans immediately following Hurricane Katrina. His camera produced the most damning evidence of alleged police wrongdoing. While driving between St. Bernard Highway and Judge Perez Drive near Chalmette, David, along with his coworker and staff photographer Tom Cox, had stopped to help a dog but were dismayed at what happened next. Two people in a Jeep and two officers in the back of a pickup truck drove to where David and Tom had parked and were giving water to the dog. Otherwise, David said, he and Tom would have driven off and wouldn't have seen the dog shot to death. Instead, they ended up being witnesses. Right in front of them, deputies killed the dog they had been helping, David said.

The Pulitzer Prize–winning photographer then filmed other events. On the raw tape, David said, the shootings of eight or nine other dogs can be heard—first gunfire and then yipping. Also disturbing was the admission by then Sergeant Mike Minton that he had, in fact, killed dogs by shooting them.

When the sergeant noticed David's camera, he jumped in front of David and asked what was going on. David identified himself as being with the paper and asked the officer about the shootings. Sergeant Minton, David said, started talking on camera, with the red "on" light in plain view. "Really, it's [to] benefit a dog, really, because, you know, where's he gonna find food, where's he gonna find water, you know? So, I just looked at it as it's more humane, doing it to protect myself, but it's more humane for the dog, you know. They tried to eat us. Four days into it, [a deputy] almost got eat up by a Pit Bull."

The paper, under subpoena, turned over to the attorney general's office David's raw video footage of dogs being gunned down on the streets on September 7. The video included a sheriff's deputy shooting two dogs.

Sergeant Minton, who was suspended by his department after an edited version of the conversation was posted on the *Dallas Morning News* Web site, resigned from his post. The video contained enough evidence for the attorney general's office to continue its investigation, with a grand jury eventually indicting and charging Minton with a sundry of felony animal cruelty counts. Also indicted by the same grand jury was Clifford "Chip" Englande, a sergeant who, after the indictment, was assigned to administrative duties. Both men, who face up to ten years in prison if convicted, pleaded innocent. Minton's attorney has said that his client shot only dogs that were dangerous.

According to Assistant Attorney General Mimi Hunley, for those dogs shot on the street, the attorney general's office had the evidence of David Leeson's film. For the dogs and cats shot inside the schools, proof lay in the video footage CNN's news crew took when Anderson Cooper went there with animal abuse investigator Mark Steinway from Pasado Rescue. Anderson, looking subdued, began his newscast by telling viewers that they wouldn't be able to tell from outside the innocuous-looking Beauregard Middle School, with its colonial-style architecture, that a slaughter had taken place inside.

On September 30, when Anderson and Mark arrived at the middle school, just fourteen dead animals remained, far fewer than Christopher Acosta had counted when he had been there two weeks earlier. Mark also videotaped the bodies found at the elementary and high schools, for a total of thirty-three dogs and cats found dead. The Pasado rescue group covered the costs of necropsies (animal autopsies) for these animals and handed over the results to the attorney general's office.

At a pretrial hearing, animal rights activists gathered outside the state district courthouse in Chalmette, some holding signs that read JAIL TIME FOR ANIMAL CRUELTY. Other animal proponents sat in on the proceeding.

Our group was horrified by what had happened. A team from Best Friends had gone to St. Bernard High School in the first days after animal rescue groups were given the green light to enter the parish. By then, on September 20, most of the bodies had been removed. Under the bleachers on the football field, however, were three dead dogs. One uninjured dog, a Rottweiler, was sitting next to the bodies as if watching over them. The frightened male Rottweiler was leashed and walked out from under the bleachers and then taken to Camp Tylertown that night.

I was with the team that day, and we didn't inspect the bodies. We thought they'd died in the storm. In addition, CNN's report hadn't yet aired, and we didn't know that the bleachers were where the animals' remains had been stored until they were removed.

At the time, several of us commented on how many dogs and cats were running loose in just a three-block area of homes surrounding the high school. We rescued at least twenty-five pets that day alone from in and around the high school.

Volunteer Mike McCleese noted, "I can still hear the eerie silence of those streets—no sounds of machines or trucks or cars, no sounds of electricity, no children playing, no sounds of birds chirping or insects buzzing," Mike said. "The only thing I heard was the crunch of drying sludge under my boots whenever I took a step."

For photographer Clay Myers, it wasn't the silence that felt different from other rescue details he'd been on; it was the large number of loose animals: "While every neighborhood I was in had its share of shy, frightened dogs, that one by far had the most. Dogs were running at top speed away from us. They were terrified of being caught."

Mike and Clay didn't learn until afterward that the school had been a refuge where evacuees stayed with their pets for at least three days. For Mike, learning later about the shootings inside the school was disturbing. "I am horrified by this crime," he said. "To think that I stood unknowingly outside a place where so many people's beloved animals were brutally killed overwhelms me with grief and sadness. When we stood outside that school, it seemed like nothing was alive, except us—and then Clay found Angel."

Kris Wartelle, spokeswoman for the Louisiana attorney general, said publicly that she couldn't comment early on about how many officers may have been involved, except to say they had a list of deputies they were questioning in connection with the cases. Early speculation ruled out any involvement by National Guard officers. On September 29, after the bodies of animals were discovered at Sebastian Roy Elementary School on Bayou Road, St. Bernard Sheriff Jack Stephens told CNN that he was not prepared to say without reservation that it wasn't one of his officers who did it. He made a point of describing the violent acts as despicable.

About sixty people had evacuated with their pets to Beauregard Middle School, including lifetime resident Kit Bauer. She was rescued on August 29 from her attic when neighbors in a boat heard one of her dogs barking. They motored her to Beauregard, where she and her dogs spent three days. When she was forced to leave her dogs at the school, Kit wrote a note that included her cell phone number in chalk on a wall outside the classroom where she'd left her dogs. It read, "In this room are 6 adult dogs and 4 puppies. Please save them. Kit." The puppies were three-week-old Dachshunds and were still nursing. Kit left water and opened three boxes of Fruit Loops cereal for them. Out of the ten, one dog, Indy, was located two weeks after the storm at a shelter and returned to Kit. The adult dogs were shot to death. The puppies were never located.

Jodie Jones, another evacuee, also left a note at a school. She and her husband, Clay, had evacuated the Saturday after the levees broke. A half mile down Bayou Road, the Joneses left their three cats and a dog in the hands of deputies at the makeshift evacuee center at St. Bernard High School. To their horror, two of their cats were fatally shot four weeks later inside the carriers they had delivered them in. They never found their third cat. All were ten to twelve years old.

"I asked the deputies to promise me they'd get my animals to safety," Jodie said. "They assured us nothing was going to happen to them."

Their dog, Suzie, somehow escaped being shot and was located in a foster home. "Suzie made it to California," Jodie said, but "she died three days before we were scheduled to get her. I think she died of grief." At least, Jodie said, it was comforting to know that Suzie died in a home and not at the hands of rogue officers. "I trusted the deputies," Jodie said. "It is such a shock and such a heartbreak that anybody could just shoot [those animals]."

Another lucky dog was Angel the Pit Bull, who also survived. Angel was rescued from St. Bernard High School twenty-two days after the storm. She was plucked from the second-floor library, the scene of target practice against the animals. Angel, whose real name is Sassy, was spotted by Best Friends photographer Clay Myers on September 20 as he walked across the grounds of the high school, looked up, and saw a Pit Bull staring down at him from a second-floor window. Clay walked up the grimy stairs to the second floor, and Angel, who was frightened, jumped out a window onto the roof. Clay didn't want her to jump off the roof, so he summoned dog handler Ethan Gurney, also with the team that day, to help. Ethan arrived a few minutes later and was able to slip a loop lead around the dog's neck and walk her safely out of the school to the waiting transport van. Dehydrated and scared, Angel was driven to Camp Tylertown.

Angel had her twelve puppies while in a van on her way to her Houston foster home. Evacuee Jenny Fourcade, who had been at the school with Angel's owner, read her story and saw a photo of Angel on the Best Friends Web site. She left a comment, saying the dog's name was Sassy, and then notified the dog's person. Once a positive identification was made with the owner, arrangements began for Angel to go home. Her person learned that Angel had given birth to twelve puppies and that ten survived and were adopted out.

Today, Angel is again living in St. Bernard Parish. When she first returned home, Jane Ezell, Angel's person, took her to their old house. When they walked Angel down the street, she saw the house, perked up, and ran into the yard. Jane described it as a special moment for Angel, because it was obvious she remembered and it made her feel more secure to go home again.

Carol Hamm stayed at the high school for two days, waiting for her husband and son, who used their boat to rescue people stranded on rooftops and in attics of flooded homes. While at the high school, Carol said, "One moment [the deputies] told us we could take our pets, and the next moment they said we couldn't. My husband was still at the house with our dogs."

Her husband paddled a boat and dropped off their four dogs at Beauregard Middle School because sheriff's deputies told him to go there and that officers would take the dogs to an animal shelter for safekeeping. Then he and their son went to the high school to be with Carol. A day later they all were evacuated, thinking they'd retrieve their dogs in a few days.

A lot of residents had evacuated with their animals to St. Bernard High School, one of the other makeshift refugee centers where Angel's person had left her, and where others, like the Hamms, also left their pets, believing them to be in safe hands. "People were there with dogs, cats, and birds, too. You name it, people brought them," Carol said. "There was an old woman who wanted to take her Yorkie. The dog was so tiny, she could fit it in her purse. They made her leave it."

While still at the high school waiting to be evacuated, Carol overheard a deputy say to another officer that as soon as people left, he was going to shoot the pets. Carol and others confronted the officer. "A medic was also there," Carol said, "and he told me he wouldn't let anything happen to [the pets]."

It wasn't until September 30 that Carol returned to the middle school to look for their family pets, after she was contacted by CNN and asked to meet the TV crew there. What they found— the remains of family pets—was unspeakable. "It's the worst memory I'll ever have," Carol later said. "The bodies were being removed. It was horrible. I was crying over strangers' dogs. Only three of our dogs were in the room. We saw a Golden Retriever, two Yorkshire Terriers, all breeds, and a lot of Pits and Rotties. Some were shot running, one as he ran up the stairs. Bullet, our Husky mix, was shot in the head."

While the investigations into the shootings continued, those whose pets were either lost in the carnage or reunited with them tried to move on. Carol and her family, who now live in Temple, Texas, have been reunited with Daisy, the sole survivor among the four dogs they left at the school. Somehow, Daisy survived. Carol has her own theory, noting that Daisy "has always been an escape artist." A Best Friends team in the area picked up Daisy in late September. She, too, was taken to Camp Tylertown and then placed in foster care in Iowa. The foster family later returned her to the Hamms.

Christopher and Crystal Acosta, after living in a hotel for a couple of months, eventually moved into a FEMA trailer on their property in St. Bernard Parish while they repaired their house. Crystal had a healthy baby girl, Iceie, who was born September 1, just after Crystal had evacuated. Novocain, the dog who had been left near the barges, was reunited with the family four and a half months after the storm. His foster mom, Kim Moore, drove Novocain from Ohio to Louisiana. At the reunion, she described him as a good dog and said while she would miss him, she was happy to bring him home. And the day Christopher and his wife saw Mercedes again for the first time, Christopher was emotional, telling reporters who met him and his dog at the middle school that he loved her and was grateful to get her back. Christopher's uncle's dog, a German Shepherd, also somehow escaped from the school and was found on his porch when his person returned home.

For the pet owners not as lucky as the Acostas, returning to St. Bernard Parish was difficult. Jodie Jones returned to her home on Valentine's Day after she and her husband received keys to their FEMA trailer. She couldn't help but miss her pets. Going home brought back memories, she said. "You know how when you pull up in the driveway you're used to them barking, and when you go inside they're happy to see you?" she said. "It was like we expected to see them, but they weren't there. It's been difficult. My pets were my children. I can't get over the abuse."

Kit Bauer, who now lives out of state, won't be returning to St. Bernard Parish. "There's nothing to go back to," she said. As for the investigation into the shootings, Kit said she doesn't want to dwell on what the deputies may or may not have done. She'd known some of those officers for years and went to school with at least one of them. They took good care of her, she said, while she was at the school, and she appreciated that. Her only hope, she noted, was that her dogs hadn't suffered.

As for the legal cases against the officers charged with opening fire on the pets left in the three schools by their owners, helping with the case through his videotape was what David Leeson was trained to do. "I wasn't out looking for an ax to grind that day," said the veteran newspaper photographer. "I didn't raise a rifle that day. I raised a camera. I did what I'm supposed to do as a journalist. Journalists are the watchdogs of society. I let others judge and let the truth come out. It's gratifying to see that there are times when both the media and the system work."

17

Putting Haley First

F OR A DOG NAMED HALEY, a pending reunion with her people took on a different twist. Both her owners and her foster dad agreed that the difficult decision they were about to make was the right one for Haley.

Haley's family, Doris and Henry Wyman, searched for their dog after they evacuated. They later learned that a month after the storm, Haley, whose original name was Boo, had been found in the Lower Ninth Ward on the still-standing back porch of their battered wooden shotgun house—so named because a shotgun could fly through the open front door to the back of the house, never hitting a thing as it sailed down the long, narrow hallway. That type of construction was typical of the more affordable houses of New Orleans, but the simple structure didn't hold up well during a hurricane. The Lower Ninth Ward was left abandoned longer than other communities because so many homes in the working-class neighborhood had been flattened, and there was nothing more than debris to return to. Still, pets like Haley remained in the uninhabited Ninth Ward until they were rescued.

After Katrina, Doris said she could only imagine how Haley must have felt, alone outside the house and wondering where all the people had gone. Henry had stayed for a week upstairs in their home with Haley and their cat, Lucky, until National Guardsmen arrived and ordered him to leave. "Give me a second," Henry told them. He went back upstairs, emptied a bag of dog food, and walked out of the house without his pets. He did not want to leave, his wife explained. "It pained him to leave Boo and Lucky," Doris said—so much so that not knowing what

196

happened to their pets threw Henry into a depression for months. He didn't hold much hope that he'd ever see them again. After all, the Lower Ninth, as the district is called, was the hardest hit in the New Orleans area. Many of the homes were thrown off their cinder-block foundations and crushed by flood-waters that burst through broken levees at the nearby Industrial Canal. Doris didn't know what had happened to their rental house, their belongings, or their pets.

Then the Wymans returned home a few weeks later to find a note on the back of their house saying that their dog had been rescued and was at base camp in Tylertown, Mississippi. Their cat, however, had not been found. After the match with Haley was made, workers began to make arrangements to pick up the German Shepherd mix from her foster home in South Lion, Michigan, and return her to the Wymans in New Orleans.

However, just a couple of days before the scheduled home-coming, the Wymans reconsidered. They decided, after much discussion, to leave Haley in her foster home. "The biggest thing after all this time is knowing she is okay and that she is in a lov-ing home," Doris said in a telephone interview. "We're in an apartment and our landlord doesn't want a big dog here." Also, because they don't have a yard, "I'd hate to bring her to an inse-cure situation and have her lost again. It was terrible not know-ing where she was."

Mike Magyar, Haley's foster parent, agreed to adopt Haley. In her new home, where she's been since November 2005, she has the company of another dog, Harley, also a German Shepherd mix. Mike was fine with returning Haley to her family when that was the plan. "There was no way I would keep her from them," Mike said. "I had no problem giving her back, because she was their dog. But if they've got no place to take her to, I'm happy to keep her."

"Once we talked to Mister Mike," Doris explained, "my hus-band's whole demeanor changed because he knew she was okay.

That was the main reason my husband stayed behind. Knowing that this gentleman is going to take good care of her, that's all that matters to us. She's like a child to us. You hope they go out there in the world and that they're doing well and they're loved."

For some pets, Katrina, while devastating in so many ways, was the best thing that ever happened to them. The case of a red retriever and shepherd mix without a name whose owner had moved to Lake Charles is one example. The dog was wearing a collar with a rabies tag that led to her person. When reached, the owner described her as "a yard dog" he'd never taken the time to name; he simply referred to her as "Dog." He had no place for Dog and, without hesitation, surrendered her to Best Friends. The rescuer who retrieved her from North Claibourne and Jourdan avenues next to the Inner Harbor Navigation Canal in Orleans Parish described her as feral-like, scared, and aggressive, no doubt because of the solitary life she'd lived in a yard, not to mention having just survived a hurricane on her own. At the M*A*S*H Unit, she tested positive for heartworm, which was not uncommon for the yard dogs who were rescued.

Because she was fear-aggressive, the dog was transferred to the St. Francis Sanctuary to be treated for heartworm and begin work to increase her confidence. The dog, who was named Nicole, was put in a fifty-by-seventy-five-foot grassy run with Jordan, a shy Beagle also rescued from Katrina. Nicole and Jordan are able to get out of their run on the fifty-acre St. Francis property, which is fenced, and a few nights a week they "escape" by digging under the fence. Then they spend the rest of the night chasing field mice. "As soon as the caregivers arrive at work the next morning," said St. Francis's Heidi Krupp, "Nicole and Jordan hurry back, go under the fence, and return to their run." Caregivers regularly fill the holes the pair digs, but they eventually make it out of their run again. "It's become a regular routine for them," Heidi explained.

Today, Nicole—once called Dog—still lives at St. Francis and, Heidi reports, is still buddies with Jordan.

In a case similar to that of Haley, a Golden Retriever named Sassy was about to be reunited a month after the storm when her owners gave her up. The couple from New Orleans were contacted using a phone number, included on the dog's tag, that was put back into service three weeks after the storm. The foster mom, Anne Park, was attached to Sassy, but more importantly, Anne said, the previously shy Sassy had adjusted well in her Colorado home. She was used to running and playing on their property with two other dogs. Anne called the lost-and-found office at base camp.

"Do you think the owners will let me keep her?" she asked.

"It won't hurt to try," she was told.

When the original owner was called, he said he had already thought about not taking her back because he didn't want to see Sassy go back to living outdoors again.

Before the storm, Sassy lived in the couple's backyard because, the husband explained, his wife didn't like fleas or fur in their home. He said he'd hate to see Sassy survive Katrina only to live out back again. But the decision to either keep or surrender Sassy, he said, was also his wife's. He planned to discuss it with her and let us know. About an hour later, he called back to say he and his wife had agreed that they wanted what was best for Sassy and that they wanted her to remain in Colorado.

Today, Sassy—now called Loxi—lives on thirty-five acres with four horses. "She runs her entire body down the length of the fence while the horses follow her," Anne said. "She itches and groans and loves it. Then she'll turn around and do the other side with the horses turning around and following her. It's hilarious."

Anne and her husband adopted another Katrina dog, an Akita named Camelot. The two also live with a Greyhound and two Newfoundland dogs. "Loxi's the instigator of play with two huge Newfies and a big Akita and a Greyhound, and usually the one that takes the roughest part of the play with pleasure," Anne said. "My Newfie Rope will run up to her, bump her, and roll her completely over numerous times. She has such a good nature and goes back for more.

"She gets along great with all dogs and humans, and we couldn't be happier with her."

In another case, an at-risk Great Dane posed ongoing, expensive medical care for her owner, who was still displaced. While her person loved her, she put the dog's well-being first.

Gracie, a beautiful but skinny Great Dane, was rescued on September 12, 2005, from a street in Gretna on the west bank of the Mississippi River just east of uptown New Orleans. Gracie needed long-term medical care. When the merle-colored dog, with her bluish-gray coat streaked with black and white, went through the admissions process at Camp Tylertown, animal-care manager Sherry Woodard noticed immediately that she was panting heavily. Worried that Gracie might overheat, Sherry walked her to volunteer Clay Myers' personal RV, which Clay drove from Utah to Mississippi, and asked if Gracie could stay inside his air-conditioned quarters. "Bring her in," Clay told her. Sherry had already given Clay a snake and a small Beagle who was crated to keep in the RV and out of the Mississippi heat.

When Gracie walked into the RV, "she looked around, plopped down, and put her head on my feet," Clay said. "I could tell she was saying, 'Thank you' because the RV was quiet, cool, and like home. She really touched me; she was so delicate."

After a couple of days, Clay said, "she went off to New York."

Marcello Forte with Animal Haven, a rescue group in the urban neighborhood of Flushing in the New York City borough of Queens, was at base camp when Gracie arrived. He took the grossly underweight Great Dane back with him to his shelter.

Once there, she was diagnosed with and treated for Addison's disease, an adrenal insufficiency, and then placed with a family in upstate New York.

Meanwhile, her owner, upon learning that rescued animals had been taken to Camp Tylertown, drove there on a late September afternoon looking for her dog. She was told that Gracie had been placed in foster care but that arrangements would be made to deliver her back home to New Orleans. Once her person learned that Gracie had been diagnosed with Addison's disease and was undergoing treatment, however, she decided, after discussing the matter with the foster group, to leave Gracie in her new home and allow the foster family to adopt her.

Gracie slowly gained the weight she had lost and is thriving at home with her housemates, a pair of Labrador Retrievers. Marcello reports that Gracie "settled into her new home with the rest of her playmates" and "truly is a gentle giant that would rather be on your lap or resting her head on your favorite pillow."

18

Over the Rainbow Bridge

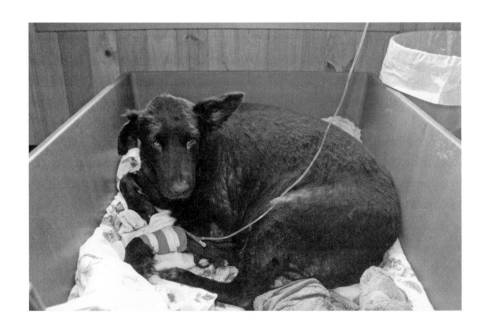

FIVE DOGS—Silver, an aging Bulldog; Big Mama, an obese Lab so fat she couldn't walk; MacKenzie, a frightfully thin English Bull Terrier; Tilly, an old Boxer with cancer; and Jellybean, a Pit Bull with severe heartworm—had one thing in common: all found homes where their adopters doted on them. Nevertheless, once there, they didn't make it. Somehow these pets knew their days were numbered and waited until they found homes before crossing over the Rainbow Bridge.

Silver—who had ID number BF-01 and the distinction of being the first dog rescued by Best Friends—died four weeks after he went home. He was walking in his backyard with his foster mom and two other dogs when he simply sat down and passed away. Even with heartworm disease, Silver, who was at least twelve years old, was a big, lovable Bulldog who never let his illness get him down. While at Camp Tylertown, Silver had the run of the office and took turns sitting next to volunteers as they worked, often plopping himself on top of their feet and looking up at them to say hello.

When I said good-bye to Silver on September 14, 2005, the day he went to his new home, I sat down on the floor with him. He climbed up on my lap and reached up so he could give me a kiss.

Silver became the office mascot after Sherry Woodard, who oversaw animal care at Camp Tylertown, walked him inside to get him out of the heat. A few days later, volunteer Molly Golston fostered Silver, who had a tricolored, marble-streaked coat, and then took him home with her to Wake Forest, North Carolina.

On October 18, a little over a month later, Silver walked onto the grass in the backyard just like he did every morning. This time, there was a different outcome. Without any warning that he wasn't doing well, he passed away.

"He lay down in the yard, and the dogs and I sat with him," Molly said. "It was the sweetest and saddest thing. I am so happy I brought him home and had him for the time I did. He was happy here."

Just when volunteers thought they had seen it all, a dog they would call Big Mama arrived at base camp on September 16. With her were two other dogs: Dad, a Chow, and Scooter, a young Chow-Lab mix. A rescue team found the three dogs in a house, submerged except for their heads in muddy water and debris. All three welcomed the rescuers and didn't put up a fight when they were pulled from the muck to safety. When the dogs arrived at camp, Big Mama was the first pet lifted out of the transport van. "I remember the gasps," said volunteer Kelli LeBlanc with the Westminster Pet Sanctuary, a small rescue group in Ottawa, Ontario, Canada. "We were not even sure if she was really a dog at that point, she was so big. She was whisked away to emergency very quickly."

Dad was wet and tired, and his matted fur was so filthy from the sludge that he was shaved by a groomer first thing the next day. After a physical examination, his admissions paperwork included the notation that he was panting, weak, and depressed. Scooter was taken under the wing of Kelli and her friends from the Canadian rescue group, who took him for walks and let him stay in their tent at night.

Big Mama was a black Flat-Coated Retriever with a friendly disposition. The problem was that she could barely walk because she was eighty pounds overweight. To make matters worse, she had been bred too many times.

Believed to be the most obese dog rescued from New Orleans, Big Mama recuperated in the M*A*S*H Unit at Camp Tylertown. Volunteers put her in a wagon every day and pulled her around the yard so she could get fresh air. They lifted her by draping a beach towel under her belly and using it as a sling to support her. Slowly, she improved. Volunteers, including Kelli (who had brought her in), regularly visited with her in the triage building. "I remember when I went in and saw Big Mama stand up for the first time," Kelli said. "I cried tears of joy. She was a beautiful girl who would not give up without a fight. There were too many of us pulling for her."

The three former housemates—Big Mama, Dad, and Scooter—were fostered out to volunteer veterinarian Janine Pepine, who helped care for them at base camp before she drove them to her hospital, Tender Loving Care, in Medina, Ohio.

In late November 2005, Big Mama had surgery for a pre-existing uterine infection. Afterward, her health deteriorated. Her kidneys failed, and she passed away on December 1.

"I still think about her," Kelli said about Big Mama. Scooter and Dad found new homes in the Medina area.

Some pets had a better chance of survival than others. For a Bull Terrier named MacKenzie, the odds were against her from the start. She arrived at Camp Tylertown emaciated and with a fungus growing all over her body. When the rescue team found her in Orleans Parish near Lake Pontchartrain, she was in a locked garage, sitting on a workbench with a padlocked chain around her neck. It was September 29, which meant that she'd been trapped in the garage, which had bars on the windows, for at least thirty days. An independent rescue team, who had heard her whimpering, made it through the door, cut the chain from her neck, and rushed her to the Lamar-Dixon shelter in Gonzales. A couple of days later volunteers took her to Camp Tylertown's M*A*S*H Unit because she needed more medical care than they could give her. As it turned out, on top of everything else wrong with her, MacKenzie also had a bad case of heartworm infestation, plus her abdomen was bloated because of intestinal worms.

She went home with the HOPE Safehouse group to Racine, Wisconsin. She was too weak to undergo heartworm treatment until she was stabilized. Even so, MacKenzie, who was partially blind, was protective of her kennel until she recognized the voices of people she knew.

Regular updates about MacKenzie were posted on the group's Web site, including details about her weight gain and gradual health improvements. At the organization's temporary shelter, she took daily walks. Just a handful of volunteers could walk her, however, because she still occasionally became territorial in her kennel.

Her owner was found, and workers spoke with him a few times, but while arrangements were being made to safely transport her home, she developed pneumonia. MacKenzie passed away shortly after.

Sherry Woodard had spent time with the white Bull Terrier while she was in the triage area at Camp Tylertown. Her large kennel had been on the porch at Kitty City, in the shade, in part so she would get used to being around people and get past her kennel possessiveness. Volunteers during breaks would sit outside her kennel carefully petting her and talking softly to her so she'd become accustomed to their voices. Sherry was one of the few who could sit for long periods, without MacKenzie growling at her. Volunteers watched as MacKenzie cuddled up to Sherry.

The intensity of Hurricane Katrina created a survival-of-the-fittest situation, and not many older pets made it. Most of the survivors were anywhere from six months to five years old. So stumbling across an aging dog came as a surprise to the pair who rescued Tilly, a Boxer who was about twelve. She went to live with Dana Herman of Minnesota, who helped rescue her from under a house in the town of Gentilly (which is why Dana named her Tilly).

Dana and volunteer Ken Ray had taken an address list with them into the field that day in mid-September. The addresses were from people asking for someone to check on their animals. What Dana and Ken found wasn't good. Rescuing Tilly was the high point of the day.

"This was the worst day," Dana said. "We went to the addresses. Most of the animals we found were dead or not there. There was supposed to be a Yorkie in an attic. The crate was there, but the crate door was open and the dog was gone. It was so surreal, because the stairs to the attic were pulled down (leading from the attic to the first floor) and all the doors and windows to the house were locked. There was no way for the dog to get out, and no one had been inside the house yet. The water hadn't gone to the attic, but it was so hot up there."

The pair went to another house, whose residents had left a phone message asking Best Friends rescuers to break in to find their pets. When Ken and Dana arrived at the house, bars were on all the windows except for the bathroom. "It was supposed to have two Australian Shepherds and three cats inside," she said.

As Ken pushed her up and through the unbarred window, Dana caught sight of a dog. "Right as Ken was about to push me through the window, I saw this little face under the foundation of the house next door," she said. "I told Ken, 'There's a Boxer!' He said we had to go inside the house first."

When Dana jumped down into the bathroom, the room was full of sludge. She stepped out of the bathroom and "there were the two Australian Shepherds. They were dead for we don't know how long. There was a cat door. Hopefully, the three cats got out."

She had to step over the bodies to open the front door for Ken, and they searched the rest of the house to make sure the cats weren't still inside. "We went outside and I said, 'We have to get that little Boxer.' She was curled up under the house, and we pulled her out. She was a senior dog. She was so thin, and she had tumors all over her. One was hanging from her side that was bigger than a softball." But she was alive.

That night, Dana stayed behind at base camp, and Ken drove the Boxer home to Alabama with him. The dog then went to

Minnesota once Dana returned home a few days later. Animal Ark, the group with which Dana had traveled to Camp Tylertown, posted Tilly's photo and identifiers on Petfinder's Web site.

Later, Animal Ark was contacted by a volunteer who put Dana in touch with a family searching for an older Boxer. "We thought we'd found her owner," Dana said. "I spoke to the people and sent them pictures. The location was nearby."

Before that, however, Dana had taken Tilly to her veterinarian to have a large tumor on her spleen removed. Tilly also was having seizures and was under veterinary care for that, too.

When the potential owners saw the photos of Tilly, they told Dana they thought she was their dog, who was named Deja.

"I still don't know for sure if it was her, but it might have been," Dana said. "They told me she had tumors. I spoke to the daughter and the mom. It sounded like they wanted her back, but they wanted to fly her right back. They needed to wait until she recovered because she had just undergone surgery. My vet called their vet, and then I never heard from them again."

Tilly was diagnosed with hemangiosarcoma, an aggressive cancer of the blood vessel cells.

For Dana, it was Tilly who saved *her* on that hot September day.

"It was sad," she said. "We didn't find any animals alive except for Tilly. She's the one who helped me. I'm lucky I found her that day."

Tilly lived with Dana and her husband for a total of nine months, four of which were after the tumor was removed.

"She was the sweetest thing in the world," Dana said. "She was just perfect. We didn't even have her a year, but I'm glad she didn't die under the house. At our house she would come out in the morning after waking up, and she would do these dive-bomb rolls. She would get so silly. She got along great with dogs, cats, people, kids, everyone. She was a special little dog."

What Tilly and the other pets of Katrina seemed to want the most was to be in a home and, just like the two-legged Katrina refugees, to return to their lives as they were before the storm. For those pets who weren't reunited with their people, the next-best thing was a new home. Silver, Big Mama, MacKenzie, and Tilly did not die homeless or alone on the streets of New Orleans. They went home first.

It was the same for Jellybean. Terrie Spease knew how sick the light-brown, red-nosed Pit Bull was, but she had no idea he would go so quickly. Seven days after Jellybean arrived at Terrie's home, he died of heart failure. Terrie was devastated.

She had agreed to foster Jellybean—a handsome dog who was rescued with two chickens and a rooster in Central City—even though she was fully aware that he hadn't been well at base camp, that he was in heart failure and needed hospice care in a quiet home environment. Terrie, a hospice nurse, was just the right person for the job.

She had met Jellybean during her first tour at base camp and later kicked herself for not taking him home sooner. She had gone home and couldn't stop thinking about him. Deep down, though, she knew he'd been on a gradual downhill slope, no doubt even before he was rescued, and that what he needed was, indeed, hospice care.

While in his new home, Jellybean ran in the yard and hid toys. Best of all, Terrie reported, he loved sleeping on her sofa. But one day in particular with Jellybean stands out. "My favorite moment with him was about an hour after getting here," Terrie said. "I took him walking in the field across from my house, and he lay down almost immediately and began to roll. He seemed to roll around forever.

"To me, he was ridding himself of the tragedy and heartache of the previous months. He was cleansing himself to start fresh. He was a big, scary-looking dog, but I believe deep inside he saw himself as a Poodle—a tiny, couch-loving Poodle."

Those who fostered Katrina pets who passed away sooner than anticipated all said the physical distance they were able to put between Hurricane Katrina and a comfortable home for these pets was enough to make the pain of losing them worthwhile.

19

Picking Up the Pieces

FOR SOME HURRICANE VICTIMS, the biggest losses from the storm were their pets. It was that way for Barbara Seals. She knew that if she could get her Prince back, her family, who'd already lost two loved ones, would be one step closer to being whole again, one step closer to picking up the pieces. Likewise, for the new family of a dog named Cheesecake, patiently working through a lengthy adjustment period for the frightened dog was their way of helping one canine hurricane victim. And for artist Cyrus Mejia, a former New Orleans resident, creating a work of art in memory of the volunteers who'd put their lives on hold to help the pet victims was his contribution to the cause.

All Barbara Seals wanted in the aftermath of Hurricane Katrina was Prince, the dog she'd lost to the storm. On Thanksgiving weekend in 2005, I returned to New Orleans and stopped at a Walgreens drugstore on South Claiborne Avenue in Carrollton, the only store open for miles. It still had boarded-up windows, and only part of the store was stocked with merchandise. Standing at the door waiting outside for her niece was Barbara, along with a black Cocker Spaniel named Princess. I bent down to say hello to the dog, and Barbara began telling me her story. I then took a photo of Barbara and Princess and offered to write a story about them for the Best Friends Web site.

Before the storm, Barbara had left her other dog, Prince, with her fiancé, Clarence Smith, at his apartment on Rampart Street, a historic neighborhood in the Lower Ninth Ward. Clarence stayed behind after the storm to be with Prince. When he was ordered at gunpoint to evacuate a few days later, he left Prince in an apartment in the building with a couple of other dogs. When he returned to retrieve Barbara's dog after he was allowed in two weeks later, a sign on the door said that Prince and the other dogs had been picked up by animal control and taken to the Louisiana SPCA. Clarence and Barbara went to the shelter twice but were told that there was no record of Prince. They were advised to go online to the Petfinder Web site to find him. They visited the site for weeks to no avail, searching for a Cocker Spaniel who looked like Prince.

Barbara, who'd kept Prince's littermate, Princess, with her when she evacuated, searched high and low for Prince. Her two daughters posted a notice on Petfinder and searched every posting on the site for his breed, "Cocker Spaniel," with no luck. They went to shelters. Still no luck.

What they didn't know was that Prince had been picked up from Clarence's apartment on September 18, transferred first to the Lamar-Dixon shelter, and then moved again to another local shelter. From there, he was flown with a group of dogs to the Last Chance Ranch Equine Rescue in Pennsylvania. That group placed Prince in a home with foster mom Melanie Bailey.

Barbara also didn't know that a problem with the Petfinder listing—an error that listed Prince as a Poodle instead of a Cocker Spaniel—was the reason she couldn't locate him among the thousands of online dog listings. Melanie feared that Prince's family was not going to be able to find him, so she contacted the group who gave him to her and sent an e-mail that she believed was addressed to Petfinder. Instead, it went to the Stealth Volunteers, a group that helps match lost animals with their people. It was Melanie's e-mail sent to the wrong person that ultimately led Barbara to Prince, because a Stealth Volunteer held onto that e-mail.

Melanie knew as soon as she fostered Prince, beginning on October 19, 2005, that he had been in someone's home and had been loved, which was why she was persistent in making sure information about the dog was accurate on Petfinder. When he was rescued, it appeared that the buff-colored Cocker Spaniel had been recently groomed, plus he jumped up on the sofa to sleep—both indicators he had been cared for and was someone's indoor pet.

When my story about Barbara's search for Prince ran on the Best Friends Web site, Stealth Volunteers, including Robin Siegel and Carla Jennings, recalled Melanie's e-mail, which they still had in their computer archives. Robin quickly sent an e-mail to Best Friends saying she thought she knew where Prince was living, based on Melanie's earlier e-mail, and starting the process of getting Prince back home. Melanie was contacted and sent Barbara recent photos, and Barbara positively identified the dog as Prince.

Learning that Prince had been rescued "was the best news I've had since this whole thing happened," said Barbara. "So many people here need encouragement. They don't know whether their friends and family are living or not. I've been talking about Prince so much to the church. If I could just find him, that would help put things back together again. I thank God he had an angel looking over him."

For Cheesecake, it wasn't as simple as just going home. Prince had adjusted well first to his foster home and then to his original home. But Cheesecake was a frightened and sometimes possessive Pit Bull mix, and it took months for her to finally settle into life in her new home.

Life in the aftermath of Katrina wasn't easy for Cheesecake. She was found hiding in front of a house behind a large bush. Jill Garcia and her extended family—all nine of them—discovered Cheesecake shortly after they returned to their home in Metairie, a suburb of New Orleans. That was forty-five days after the storm. Jill was outside when her own dog started barking, so she walked closer to her. Something moved.

Thinking it was a raccoon, Jill called out to a neighbor to walk across her yard with her. Then a dog ran out from behind a bush in a yard across the street and jumped over a high fence into the next yard, and then into yet another yard. It looked to Jill as if the dog had taken off and was gone. The next day, however, the dog walked into the middle of the cul-de-sac and stood there, looking at Jill. Jill threw her a treat, and the stray took off again.

She left out food and water, and gradually Cheesecake became braver and began warming up to the family. On the fourth day, the Garcias opened their front door, and Cheesecake ran inside.

Jill's family named the shy dog Spook, partly because they first discovered her the day before Halloween and also because she was so skittish. But she was becoming possessive of Jill and started to growl at the other dog in the house. Additionally, she was territorial, especially toward the mail carrier.

Jill posted fliers in her neighborhood and knocked on doors, hoping to find the dog's owner, but no one had seen her before. Because Jill's household was large and the dog was having a difficult time adjusting, she took her to Celebration Station, the Best Friends temporary triage center where she was eventually adopted out.

No longer named Spook, Cheesecake currently is living with the Smith family in Prattville, Alabama. Rob and Kim Smith adopted her in February 2006.

Lucky for Cheesecake, the family was patient with her lingering skittishness after they took her home. Rob and Kim were determined to make it work, especially because their three children adored Cheesecake, naming her that because her coloring reminded them of the dessert. At first, Cheesecake was territorial with their Dachshund, Seymour. She showed her teeth to him when he went near family members she was playing with. With time, as Cheesecake became more attached to Seymour, that behavior disappeared.

The dogs are now the best of friends, sleeping together and playing nonstop. While the family has a seven-foot fence around the property, so far Cheesecake has not shown any desire to jump it and run away. Like so many other Katrina dogs and cats, she appears grateful and seems to know a good thing when she sees it.

Many other pets like Cheesecake went into new homes instead of being reunited with their original people. Their paperwork and photos filled volumes of binders at Camp Tylertown. Thumbing through the sheets of paper, it was difficult to not wonder where their families had gone. We now know that many neighborhoods were so decimated that their owners didn't make it out, or they were evacuated to Arkansas, Texas, and even Utah, never to return to their hometown of New Orleans.

For Cyrus Mejia, resident artist and one of the founders of the Best Friends sanctuary, seeing the voluminous paperwork at Camp Tylertown triggered his idea for an ambitious piece of artwork.

"All the animals that came through Best Friends' rescue center were photographed and documented with one of these forms," Cyrus said. He said to himself, *I'm going to turn them into art.* And he did.

On August 29, 2007, on the second anniversary of the day Katrina made landfall on the Gulf Coast, the finished art project—a boat called *Ark*—was unveiled to a crowd that had volunteered to help the stranded animals in the aftermath of the storm. I was there for the unveiling. The sound of water lapping against a shore played on a CD as attendees walked around the suspended *Ark*, recognizing photos of fellow volunteers and the pets they helped at both Camp Tylertown and the Celebration Station triage center. It was cathartic seeing the intake papers as part of the boat's surface instead of in binders. My Katrina foster dog, Mia, was included.

Cyrus and his wife, Anne, also a founder at Best Friends, ran the hurricane command center from the Utah sanctuary. During November 2005, however, they served as base camp managers at Tylertown, and that's when Cyrus first saw the animal admission forms. "Having lived there I'm sure added a dimension to the emotion involved," he said. "My mom was born and raised a few miles outside of Tylertown. I still have family in the area; I have cousins who lost their homes."

Before he started the project, however, it took a year for Cyrus to digest the devastation left in Katrina's wake. It was a period of mourning in a sense for a man who was born in New Orleans and spent much of his youth in Louisiana and Mississippi.

He explained that his purpose with *Ark* was to capture the fear, sadness, grief, and relief experienced by rescue teams in boats, the hundreds of volunteers on the ground, and the animals they saved through nearly nine months of work in post-Katrina New Orleans. He invited many of the volunteers who helped rescue and care for the displaced pets to send in their personal photographs. Those photos were included as part of the collage.

Ark began with a stretched canvas over a wood frame, which is a replica of the flat-bottomed jon boats used in the water rescues in the first fifteen days following Hurricane Katrina. Cyrus covered the surface with hundreds of copies of admission forms used to record information about rescued pets. He glued photographs of both rescued animals and volunteers onto the boat's surface, along with pet food and kitty litter bags cut into the shapes of dogs and cats. The bottom of the jon boat is covered with maps of the flood-ravaged areas of New Orleans, similar to the maps used by rescuers as they made their way through the flooded streets. Also included in the collage are satellite maps of the storm itself. A mirror under the installation makes the underbelly of the boat easy for viewers to see.

Cyrus finished off *Ark* by painting the eye of a hurricane swirling throughout the surface of the boat. The work was then covered in varnish.

The finished piece, he said, is a labor of love. "I think it's possible for physical items to retain emotion," Cyrus said. "I wanted to capture that energy and presence in this work."

The piece commemorates the heroic work performed by hundreds of volunteers and Best Friends staffers who "answered the call, put their lives on hold, and went to save the animals lost in Katrina's wake."

With his artwork, he often returns "to the notion that physical objects can . . . trigger forgotten feelings." That's how he felt about the paperwork for each rescued animal.

For Cyrus, the purpose of *Ark* was not only as a work of art; the collage-covered boat was also meant as a vehicle, a symbol of healing and moving on.

Katrina's impact on the people of the Gulf Coast was traumatic. The storm's impact on pets continued for months; in some cases, for a year or more. Animal lovers across the nation offered their support through donations of food and supplies. Despite limited resources, despite being separated from their families and pets for months, and despite facing obstacle upon obstacle, the people of New Orleans who returned to their homes were determined to rebuild their city.

Residents continue to pick up the pieces, putting their houses and their lives back together. While there was little help from local, state, and federal governments, Americans showed up in droves ready to help their fellow citizens, and animal rescue groups rushed to the area to rescue pets and keep them safe until they could return to the Big Easy. Despite the generosity of many people, though, some pets are still waiting to go home.

Katrina also changed people's values. Instead of material things, most of which were lost in the rubble of the storm, what was important to many were their family members and their pets. That mantra was repeated daily at animal rescue centers: *If only I can find my cat, I'll be okay.*

It was the same for Barbara Seales: *If I can get Prince back, it will help my family recover.* Prince was returned in time for Barbara's birthday and for Christmas 2005. She'd lost her daughter-in-law and her fifteen-year-old grandson in the storm. Their bodies were found twenty yards from each other on Thanksgiving 2005. Prince's return was something for the Seales family to celebrate. "The grandkids are enjoying Prince and Princess," Barbara said. "We know how lucky we are to have Prince home."

20

Lessons Learned

A FTER THE BREACH OF THE LEVEES separating the lower Mississippi River from the below-sea-level bowl of New Orleans, days turned into weeks and the pets of Katrina were forced to fend for themselves in the aftermath of the flooding. Then, in late September, Hurricane Rita hit the region, leaving some neighborhoods underwater for seven more days and stranding even more pets. Many animals were left on streets, inside homes, in yards behind fences with no way to escape, and in garages, sheds, attics, apartments, and offices.

Those on the ground in the Gulf Coast region, as well as refugees who fled the area, learned the hard way that people don't want to evacuate without their pets. When Katrina and Rita hit, many did so under duress.

Still, the pets' spirits soared above the rising floodwaters, and the hope of once again seeing their people kept them alive against terrible odds. Despite those odds, thousands braved the storms and survived. The pets lived not only without food or water but also without the companionship and care of their guardians. For the first time, the mainstream media covered that extraordinary bond between people and their pets. Haunting images flooded the airwaves: stranded humans and animals wandered aimlessly with no food or water.

Because of those images, people from across the United States and Canada arrived in droves to save the animals from the murky standing water and, later, the muck-covered streets. Then extraordinary efforts were made to reunite them with their families. More still, however, were never rescued, or the groups that did rescue them didn't have the means or the paperwork to track them, so those animals were never reunited with their people.

As a result, Hurricane Katrina was a wake-up call with a resounding message: along with people, pets also need to be protected during a disaster. What came out of the televised images, as the world watched in horror, was the vow never to let it be repeated. Katrina proved that people need to be prepared, from individuals putting identifying tags on their pets' collars or microchipping them to cat owners keeping crates on hand to government officials at all levels mandating provisions for not only humans but their pets.

Since Hurricane Katrina, state and federal legislation has been passed that requires animal shelters to be included in government disaster plans. On the national level, in a groundbreaking federal bill, leaving pets behind and thereby separating them from their humans is now unacceptable. With the sweep of a pen, Congress put the nation one step closer to protecting the health and well-being of pets in future disasters.

A congressional caucus is doing its part, as well. On September 20, 2005, Michael Mountain, president of Best Friends, met in Washington, D.C., with a group of lawmakers who make up the bipartisan Congressional Caucus for Animals. Members of the caucus asked major rescue organizations, including Best Friends, to let them know how the overall Katrina animal rescue was going—which Best Friends and the others were, at that moment, entrenched in—how interactions with the federal government were working, and how things could work better in future emergencies. The request was a positive sign that Congress was paying attention.

Of those pets reluctantly abandoned during Katrina, Best Friends rescued about 7,000, reuniting more than 15 percent. Together, all the animal groups and individuals in the area rescued roughly 20,000 animals from an estimated 100,000 to 250,000 left stranded in the New Orleans area.

Doing its part to create a solution, the next year Best Friends invited volunteers from a variety of organizations to join in a three-day roundtable discussion to help plan for the next catastrophe. At the opening meeting, Paul Berry, now CEO of Best Friends, emphasized that disasters aren't isolated to hurricanes. Disasters also include mudslides, tornadoes, wildfires, earthquakes, tsunamis, and whatever else comes along. The plan, he said, is to get disaster response right over time. Participants broke into discussion groups of five to ten people to develop strategies, tactics, and protocols to best respond in the future. In the end, each group came up with comprehensive ideas, vision statements, and outlines, all in preparation for the next big one.

The roundtable discussions were a precursor to the 2007 hands-on, four-day, outdoor rapid-response training session in Angel Canyon on the Best Friends sanctuary grounds. A hundred volunteers from thirty-one states and Canada went through the first annual real-life exercises for animal admissions, base camp operations, and FEMA-like procedures. A mock base camp was set up in a desert section on the thirty-three-thousand-acre sanctuary grounds. Volunteers were self-sufficient; they brought their own food, tents, and solar showers and set up in a remote area of the sanctuary in Angel Canyon, located about thirty miles southeast of Zion National Park.

In the days and weeks following hurricanes Katrina and Rita, accurate information, especially about what was happening to and for the animals, was hard to come by. That's where a coalition comes into play, to ensure that the next rescue of animals is more organized.

After Katrina, major national animal organizations got together to see if they could coordinate their resources for future disasters and to offer FEMA and state emergency managers a one-stop shop to address animals' needs for the next disaster.

With that in mind, Best Friends signed on with the coalition of the largest animal welfare groups in the nation. Representatives from those groups met at the Best Friends sanctuary as a formal step in the process of forming the coalition, whose aim is to work together when a disaster strikes and animals are in jeopardy. Also discussed was gaining access to disaster zones. Whereas Best Friends had an agreement after Katrina with Jefferson Parish Animal Control giving its rescue teams access, groups that had no such agreement were denied access. Had they been allowed in, even more animals could have been saved. In the future, because the coalition is working in concert with FEMA officials, a coordinated effort with full access to a disaster area will help teams search for and rescue pets in a timely fashion.

Best Friends' rapid response manager Rich Crook emphasized the importance of pulling the individual groups together so that the organizations have a plan in place when another disaster occurs.

The joint group—the National Animal Rescue and Sheltering Coalition, or NARSC, as it's being called—includes representatives from the American Humane Association, the American Society for the Prevention of Cruelty to Animals, Code3 Associates, the Humane Society of the United States, the International Fund for Animal Welfare, the National Animal Control Association, the Society of Animal Welfare Administration, United Animal Nations, and Best Friends Animal Society.

After leaving Camp Tylertown in late November 2005, I returned to the Gulf Coast region in January 2006, this time to spend the majority of my time in New Orleans, Waveland, and Gulfport to write an in-depth piece for *Best Friends* magazine about the status of animals still on the streets three months after Katrina. Animal control in the area at the time was reporting that the animals on the streets were simply strays and no different from any other city's homeless cats and dogs. I went there to see for myself.

What I found was disheartening. The word being sent out by trappers on the ground was that thousands of Katrina pets lost in the storm were still wandering the streets. Seeing the animals in person was shocking. They were skinny, pregnant, or injured, and they ran if you made even the slightest move toward them. Some had been on their own for so long without human contact that they had become feral-like.

I finished touring the region by visiting the handful of temporary rescue centers still set up. Some were breaking down camp. The volunteers—many of whom were trackers using humane traps and catch poles—were preparing to leave. Then I checked into a hotel in Carrollton to hunker down and write about what I had just witnessed. The hotel was packed with New Orleans families who had nowhere else to go. Of the many families I saw, only two had dogs with them.

Rich Crook, who in October 2005 took over operation of a small temporary shelter in a Winn-Dixie parking lot on Chef Menteur Highway (and was later hired by Best Friends as its rapid response manager), commented that so many animals were still on the streets or under houses that the numbers were beyond the scope of what local authorities could control. Because many of the pets were not spayed or neutered, they were reproducing on the streets, he explained, and their kittens and puppies were growing up feral. Throughout the Gulf region, Crook estimated the numbers still out there to be in the tens of thousands—and growing. And there was no place to house them once they were rounded up.

Anne Bell, director of the Southern Animal Foundation on Magazine Street, discussed the dilemma of the city that she said was now overrun with animals left behind in the storm. As she sat in the lobby of her veterinary clinic near downtown, she explained that probably 1,500 animals were in her neighborhood alone. They were, she said, people's pets. Anne summed up the rescuers' concerns: "We can't let anyone forget them."

The animals, who sat on porches, under cars, and under houses waiting for their people to return, appeared to be communicating the same thing as Rich and Anne: *Katrina isn't over.*

From what one volunteer with Animal Rescue New Orleans (ARNO) said, all evidence indicated the dogs and cats on the streets were domesticated strays and not part of a true stray or feral population, as New Orleans officials were saying at the time. In fact, many of the pets were arriving at rescue centers wearing collars and tags, allowing lost-and-found workers to reunite them with their families.

Months after the storm, scores of animals were still stuck in hurricane-torn neighborhoods, including the working-class community of Hollygrove near the border of Orleans and Jefferson parishes, not far from where Susan Norton's damaged townhouse sat. As Susan waited to be allowed back into her home, she moved into the same hotel where I was staying. People were returning to her neighborhood, she said, but a few blocks away in Hollygrove, the devastation was worse. The homes had been so heavily flooded and the damage so great that people couldn't go home.

Indeed, three months after the hurricane, Hollygrove locals and residents from similarly demolished communities still had not returned. As a result, stray pets had migrated to populated areas toward people, food, and water. The displaced animals, said Susan, who had been living in the hotel in the Garden District and driving to Carollton each day to work on her home, were heading to her neighborhood. As she arrived each day, she spotted dozens of cats, drawn to where the people were. She witnessed cats sitting on sidewalks, on porches, and under cars. She'd see an occasional dog under a house. The few residents who had returned, she noted, were feeding them.

In a particularly hard-hit area of Orleans Parish, near Bayou Street and Lake Pontchartrain, the Mutt Shack rescue group set up its center at Lake Castle Middle School. Amanda St. John, who had been running the operation without water or electricity, said she planned to stay until late December or early January, in time for the school's reopening, which meant that yet one more rescue group would be gone from the area.

It wasn't just New Orleans animals, however, that were still displaced. Even harder hit by Katrina were those living on the Mississippi Gulf. "There's still a lot of work to be done for the companion animals here on the coast," said Tara High, director of the Humane Society of South Mississippi, which is based in Gulfport. "If you ask some people in the community, they will say things are back to normal. I disagree. There are pockets of animals that were hit hard, and stray animals live there. We need professionals to come down and catch them." She said her facility couldn't take in any more because the shelter was already over its capacity. She, too, said what the animals appeared to be saying: "It's not over. We need help."

In Waveland, between Gulfport and New Orleans, "not a house is standing," said Anne Bell, who owned two homes that were flattened. "That was ground zero. There's nothing left in Waveland."

Except, that is, for the animals.

For months, Lisa Martin of In Defense of Animals in Canton, Mississippi, traveled to Waveland once a week to pick up dogs and cats captured by animal control. Then she took them to Camp Tylertown to be placed in foster care or reunited with their owners.

Lisa told the story of a Chihuahua's rescue as proof that efforts on behalf of the animals needed to continue. The tiny dog was taken from a house and reunited with his person after two and a half months spent alone in the once-flooded house. The little Chihuahua was under the covers, in bed, and still alive when rescuers discovered her, Lisa said. That's why she continued rescuing pets long after other animal rescuers had left the area, she explained. As long as the animals were there, she would rescue them.

An exit strategy was being discussed for future animal rescues, but for Katrina, no such plan was in place. Because of Hurricane Katrina, animal welfare groups now know they cannot go blindly into an area. There has to be a beginning- and an end-plan in place. Since Katrina, many animal welfare groups now provide rapid response training sessions, including the Humane Society of the United States, Code3 Associates, and Best Friends.

Collectively, two months following Katrina, rescue teams throughout the region who chose to stay were still taking in more than a hundred animals a day. "As long as there are populations coming in, the strays still need assistance," said Mark Mikelonis, a Louisiana veterinarian who practiced on the North Shore but volunteered for three days in November 2005 at Mutt Shack. "It's an overwhelming situation. It's difficult to get a good sense of when the right exit strategy would be.

"A lot of veterinarians in the area are out of work," he continued, saying he hoped they "will answer the call and volunteer. Many local vets are taking in pro bono cases. They're stepping up to the plate."

The challenge facing animal rescuers still on the ground was to keep the pets alive by feeding and watering them until they were rescued, and then, once they were off the streets, get medical care for them. Another goal was to rescue puppies and kittens before they grew up and began having babies of their own. National Guard Staff Sergeant Mark Rice, during a visit to Mutt Shack, said there were an overwhelming number of cats in Orleans Parish. He described his role as the eyes and ears of rescue groups. Should the stray cats be allowed to roam free, he said, they'd have kittens and the problem would worsen.

It had already started. During one three-day period in the months following Katrina, Best Friends took in thirty puppies, all second-generation Katrina dogs. "Is this the face of a stray dog?" asked Sherry Woodard, who oversaw kennel care for Best Friends' Camp Tylertown as she held a puppy in her arms. "If we work together as a team, we can change their lives by getting them off the streets and placing them in homes."

But just rounding up the pets wasn't a cure-all. "It's key to have a spay-neuter program," Sherry Woodard said. "If the strays go into the system at animal control, what's going to happen to them? They need to be placed in experienced foster homes. This is a huge opportunity to make a difference for animals in the entire region."

Anne Bell with the Southern Animal Foundation agreed. "Let's keep doing what we're doing—rescuing them and finding fosters."

Another problem facing displaced pets was the construction underway in many parts of the city, as bulldozer operators went where animals were still hiding. In late November 2005, in what has been dubbed the Great Trailer Park Rescue, teams were able to temporarily halt the razing of a mobile home park until frightened cats could be trapped and taken to safety. Jane Garrison, director at the time of ARNO, said her group, along with volunteers from Alley Cat Allies, successfully saved a hundred cats—thirty of which Best Friends took in—from the wrecking ball. The aging trailers were, ironically, then demolished to make way for trailers supplied by FEMA for other hurricane victims.

Also in late November 2005, Jane called on building crews to seek rescue help if they spotted dogs or cats on construction sites. Thousands of animals were out there, she said, noting she didn't think anyone could make an exact assessment as to just how many, but it was a lot. She suggested that animal control officers in the area drive around the city and see for themselves. The animals she and others were seeing on the streets had escaped the storm from their homes to get out of harm's way. With cold winter weather approaching, the pets would die. She described it as an urgency to continue helping the animals. Other rescuers agreed, saying that when they drove around at night, their headlights would catch the bright eyes of cats sitting under abandoned cars.

Maura Gallagher, a volunteer at several area animal shelters, including Camp Tylertown, spent the last week of November making food and water drops in the heavily damaged Ninth Ward. The area continued to have a National Guard presence, with armed officers planted at security checkpoints to keep out looters.

"There is such an opportunity right now to do it right for the Katrina animals," Maura said. "Why not make New Orleans an example of a humane city?"

It was that goal—to do right by the animals—that inspired long-term work throughout the region, much longer than anyone had predicted. For example, the American Society for the Prevention of Cruelty to Animals developed a major spay-neuter campaign across Louisiana and Mississippi. However, the urgency to continue rescuing came first, and that goal was to complete the rescue work that had begun in the days following Hurricane Katrina. Best Friends put out a plea in the form of a national news release, asking groups to remain in or return to the region. ARNO joined Best Friends in running the triage center called Celebration Station in a large former arcade building in Metairie, a suburb of New Orleans. Part of the emphasis was on getting pets spayed and neutered to cut down on the number of Katrina strays having puppies and kittens on the street.

Best Friends' rapid-response workers put together a plan to rescue every displaced pet they could find, said Paul Berry. Working together, the plan was to complete the final phase of the effort in two months by rescuing and adopting operations. It was the least rescuers could do for the left-behind pets of Hurricane Katrina. The final push was based at Celebration Station, which opened in late November 2005 and closed its doors on the last day of February 2006. During that final operation, an additional fifteen hundred animals were rescued and placed in homes, with a percentage reunited with their original people. Whether or not it was enough, it drove home the need for an exit plan for the next disaster. Among the animals saved during that final push was Red (whose story is told in chapter 10), the paralyzed Pit Bull who had emergency back surgery after his rescue and who would not have survived had Best Friends and ARNO not joined together at the Celebration Station triage center.

As for the government's role, just weeks before the first anniversary of Hurricane Katrina in August 2006, the plight of thousands of New Orleans residents and their pets led to a new federal law—the Pets Evacuation and Transportation Standards (PETS) Act—that requires local and state governments to include household pets in their evacuation plans. It also provides federal funding for pet-friendly refugee shelters. Because of the dire experiences of Hurricane Katrina, animal owners will not have to choose between saving their own lives and remaining in a disaster-ravaged area with their pets only to have to abandon them later. The measure sent a clear message to local and state governments that what happened in New Orleans should never happen again in America, because people will put their own lives in jeopardy to stay with their pets.

The cry was heard. During future disasters, groups and government agencies will meet to iron out plans for animal shelters to be set up next door to human shelters so that evacuees can be with their pets. Thanks to the public outcry after New Orleans refugees were forced to abandon their pets, during Hurricane Rita (which hit two weeks after Katrina) Texas officials allowed people to evacuate with their animals.

In South Lake Tahoe in late June 2007, the Angora wildfire destroyed more than two hundred fifty homes and seventy-five commercial buildings. As residents of the Northern California mountain resort evacuated, rescue groups, shelters, and veterinary clinics in the area put out the word that they would keep people's pets until residents were allowed to return to their homes and cabins. At an evacuation center erected inside the South Lake Tahoe Recreation Center Gymnasium, a place for residents' pets was set up. Then, during Southern California's October 2007 catastrophic wildfires, twenty-five hundred evacuated horses, cows, and other farm and ranch animals were housed at the Del Mar Racetrack's stables and fairgrounds, with hundreds of volunteers helping to feed, water, and walk them. And when twenty thousand residents fled their fiery communities for Qualcomm Stadium, home to the San Diego Chargers, they were allowed to take their pets with them. An additional hundred or so horses were evacuated to Mission Bay's Fiesta Island—an undeveloped five-mile-circumference park in San Diego—until residents were allowed back into their neighborhoods.

The acts of Texas and California officials—to make sure residents' pets were evacuated and attended to—gave hope to animal welfare activists that what happened to the people and pets of New Orleans will not be repeated.

In May 2006, I visited the former Camp Tylertown rescue center one last time. For nearly nine months, Pam Perez and Heidi Krupp had opened their sanctuary to the lost animals of Katrina. When base camp closed, a skeleton crew—Sherry Woodard, John Garcia, Mackenzie Garcia, Austin Soto, and Mary Lichtenberger—with a baker's dozen dogs in tow, were going home. Standing on the grounds of the camp, the mostly vacant lawns where scores of tents and campers had once stood were in stark contrast to what had been. When I returned that final time, there was a nostalgic feel about the place.

On May 10, without fanfare, the last thirteen dogs left Camp Tylertown. Included were the toughest of the tough, the most challenging of whom was Obed—goofy and playful, but unpredictable. "He'll bite," said Sherry Woodard. His original family was located, but they decided to give up the eight-year-old Lab-Pointer mix. Sherry was optimistic: "Obed can change. He just hasn't yet." It is exactly that mind-set, giving every dog a chance, that has turned around scores of dogs with training and TLC.

Another of the behavioral-issue dogs to leave the rescue center was Alex, a Rottweiler mix found in a trailer park next to a jail. Niblet, a rambunctious old black Lab mix, also was one of the last remaining dogs. So, too, was Meatball, a Rottweiler who was rescued six weeks after the hurricane, starving but still able to threaten strangers. Meatball became a favorite with the staff, especially because of his love affair with a cinder block. "He carries it around with him like a toy," Sherry said. "It's his security blanket. He tosses it around and tries to push his nose into the hole." The only dog in the bunch without behavior issues was Angel, an aging Chow-Lab mix who was returned to base camp when her new family discovered she had lung cancer.

"They're special dogs who will need special people. They're still working on their skills," said Sherry, who ran the kennels and oversaw animal care all those months. Sherry walked those remaining dogs in the yard one last time before putting them in an air-conditioned transport van heading out of Camp Tylertown.

After they left, I sat on the porch at Kitty City at St. Francis and looked out on the now-calm grounds. Except for the dogs playing in the grass just after breakfast, it was quiet. Months earlier, hustle and bustle had started at each first light and had continued well into the night. I remembered the concerned faces of the volunteers and staffers running around doing their jobs. Then it was a mini-city alive with activity.

One volunteer described the base camp like this: "Tylertown was to the animal community what Woodstock was to the music community. I'll never forget the rows and rows of kennels, tents, and cars with license plates from every state and Canada."

Without fail, new volunteers hit the ground running even before they set up their tents. Before they arrived, many weren't sure exactly what their roles would be, but as soon as they set foot on the grounds at the Camp Tylertown hurricane relief center, they fell into step and pulled their weight. One day into it and it was as if they had always been there.

The result was a remarkable collaborative effort, with work done by people from all walks of life. Nobody questioned the long hours. Everyone endured the heat and the onslaught of love bugs. People just got up, went to work, and started all over again each day. We had a common purpose: the animals.

When word rang out late at night—often past midnight—that a transport truck had arrived with more rescued animals, people pulled themselves out of bed and went to work like an army troop. No one gave it a second thought. Veterinarians and vet techs were at the ready, waiting to help the animals who needed immediate medical care.

Watching the dogs and cats come in, lost and frightened, and then witnessing them come back to life when they realized the storm was over, was something to see. The animals recognized that they were finally out of harm's way and in safe hands once more. The obvious relief on the part of the pets was what drove us.

The enormity of the storm did not hit most of us until afterward. At the time, we didn't talk about the destruction and loss of life. It simply was what it was. Everybody just hunkered down and worked their hardest for the animals. Even now, when I close my eyes I can see the hub of activity and hear the buzz, whirring like a motor, in Camp Tylertown. I can see the cats in their kennels, playing with feather toys or taking naps. I can hear their purrs as I stop at their kennels. I can see the dogs playing on the grass, being cuddled by volunteers, or sunning in their runs. I can hear them bark as a new dog is walked past. And I can still hear Red, the disabled Pit Bull, howling at Celebration Station for someone to play ball with him.

Sitting on the porch at the former Camp Tylertown so many months later, I thought about what a tremendous place the center had been. The day before, I had gone with volunteer Mary Lichtenberger when she drove Himie, the message-in-a-bottle dog (whose tale is told in chapter 6), home to the town of Violet in St. Bernard Parish. Seeing Himie, one of the early rescues, return home to Gary Karcher was a fitting ending. Just as they had for Himie, all the pieces fell into place for so many rescued dogs and cats—even parrots, lizards, ferrets, pigs, fish, spiders, and birds.

St. Francis, run by Pam and Heidi, is still an animal sanctuary, but now it is so much more. It stands as a symbol and a testament to the displaced pets of Katrina and Rita. Despite the odds, many animals survived and still more went home to their families. As good as Camp Tylertown was, along with a handful of other animal rescue shelters in the region, it can be even better next time because of the legislation now in place to help people's pets and because of what we learned from Katrina.

Camp Tylertown was indeed about the animals. I, for one, along with like-minded volunteers who converged on the region, will never forget them: Jellybean the Pit Bull, who thought he was a Toy Poodle; Big Bird the emu, who stood bravely among dogs and cats on a three-hour ride back to base camp; and Itty Bitty, the two-and-a-half-pound Chihuahua who walked tall.

Today, when I think of New Orleans, I think of them.

Appendix

Pet Disaster Preparedness

- Evacuate early. If you wait until there's a forced evacuation, transportation for your pets may not be available and you may have no choice but to leave them behind.
- If you have to leave or you are evacuated out, take your pets with you, even if you think you may be gone only a few hours. You may not be able to go back for them later.
- Keep leashes, collars, harnesses, carriers, and kennels on hand so you can easily and quickly transport your pets out of the danger area.
- Plan in advance where you will go. Make a list of pet-friendly hotels and boarding facilities with their addresses and phone numbers.
- Keep up-to-date identification tags on your pets' collars, with current phone numbers and addresses. Without these tags, there is no way for rescuers to know where the pets belong. Additionally, you can get your pets microchipped, with implanted ID numbers, as another form of identification. Keep a copy of the ID numbers so that you can report your missing pets to the ID companies.
- Keep current photos and descriptions (for example, "white paws," "one floppy ear," "clear" or "dark toenails," "white tip

on tail," or "dark muzzle") of your pets with you, in case you're separated from them. As mundane as these descriptions may seem, they can be used as identifiers to later claim your pet.

- If you do become separated from your pets, immediately post a lost-and-found notice on Internet sites, such as Petfinder (www.petfinder.org) and Craig's List (www.craigslist.org).
- Have enough pet food and fresh water on hand to last at least five days. If you have to leave your pets, make sure they have access to the food. Leave the toilet lid open in case the bowl is their only source of water.
- Keep your pets' medical records and medications on hand in a waterproof plastic envelope.
- Never tie up your pets or leave them in crates. During a flood, they may drown because you left them confined. During a fire, they won't be able to escape. Even in the absence of these two catastrophes, they may injure themselves. Those who rescued pets on the Gulf Coast tell stories about animals who could have lived had they not been tied to a porch or a fence, because the water was higher than their leashes could reach.
- For horses, have a planned evacuation route for every stall in your barn. Keep a can of spray paint on hand. You can use it to paint your phone number, preferably including a working cell number, on the horses' sides in case you have to let them loose in a field (safely out of the barn, so they're not trapped inside) or even on a street.

Acknowledgments

It often takes a village, and, in the case of saving the pets stranded in the wake of hurricanes Katrina and Rita, it took a selfless community of animal lovers from across the United States and Canada to pull off the largest animal rescue the world has ever seen.

I owe enormous gratitude to Pam Perez and Heidi Krupp, who opened not only their sanctuary gates but also their hearts to the pets of Katrina. Without them there never would have been a Camp Tylertown. Their property was a home away from home for hundreds of volunteers, including me, and for that I am grateful. To Kandra Mahé, also with St. Francis Animal Sanctuary, who made my day each morning when, no matter how tired she was, would say, "Good mornin', Miss Cathy." To this Californian, and I know to others, too, she was a daily reminder of the friendly Southern way.

I am indebted to Best Friends Animal Society, and Michael Mountain in particular, for agreeing to send me to the Gulf

Coast in the first place; I am forever thankful for having had the opportunity to report from the front lines. And to Paul Berry, who got the first boat into the storm water in record time (and Ken Ray for driving home to retrieve it), for making Best Friends the first in the water to save stranded and drowning pets.

To my boss, Carla Davis, for her unwavering faith in my reporting abilities. To Anne and Cyrus Mejia for their good humor as they held things together from the command center. To Sherry Woodard, our in-house animal whisperer, who with her soft touch was—and still is—a stellar example for us all. To Clay Myers for capturing the heartfelt moments from behind his camera. To Sean Scherer for his calm, gentle demeanor on even the most harrowing of days at base camp. To Mary Lichtenberger, Beth Montes, and Katherine Glover—the four of us girls worked elbow to elbow for four weeks in that tiny makeshift office, sharing laughter and tears; they are days I will always cherish. To Francis and Silva Battista for shaping up base camp and making it a well-oiled machine. To Faith Maloney for her steadfast moral support. To Pat Donoho, Kirsten Muthreich, Heidi Zogg, and Dr. Roger Knighton for watching over my dogs in my absence.

A special nod to Leigh and Terry Breland and Joy and Billy Woods for their Southern hospitality and for making me feel a part of their Mississippi family.

To Ali MacGraw for her beautiful words in the foreword to this book and her love for all living beings.

I am grateful to Susan Lee Cohen, my agent, for believing in the project; fellow author Norine Dresser for referring me to Susan; Pam Mourouzis, acquisitions editor at Wiley Publishing, for taking the manuscript under her wing; Lesa Grant and Susie Dempsey with Howell Book House for their enthusiasm and expertise; freelance editor Tere Stouffer, who massaged the manuscript with skill and care; Vicki Kilmer-Rinker with Best Friends for her marketing strategy; and artist, fellow biographer, and friend Paulette Frankl for suggesting that the word *pawprints* be added to the title.

To my family and friends, who provided sage counsel and friendship, including my twin sister, Cordelia Mendoza; big brother, Dr. J. Michael Scott; son, Raymond Somers Jr.; daughter-in-law, Karen Somers; grandchildren, Claire and Jake; stepsister, Nancy Whitlock; stepmother, Helen Scott; and friends Andrea Dresser, Myram Borders, Vickie Pynchon, Carolyn Oberlander, Linda and Roger Ballantyne, Chip Mosher, Matt O'Brien, Lora Shaner, Barb Davis, Candy Greene, Kristi Littrell, Fran Farrell, Lynn Tharp, Amy Wagner, Elizabeth Doyle, Karen Finklestein, Helene Silverstein, Claire Davis, Nancy Paris, Steve Miller, Charlene "Charlie" Fern, Stacie Hummell, Jim and Kathleen Kelley-Markum, Sandy and Joe Smith, Betty and Tom Kuffel, Andy Rathbone, Laura Rethoret, Wendy Burgoyne, Gloria Hill, Ellen Gilmore, Sandy Miller, Amy Abern, Christine McKellar, Charlene Rogers, Susie Duttge, Lezlie Sage, Jana de Peyer, and Denise Jenkins, who, no matter how over the top I am as an animal lover, continue to back me.

To the many volunteers and Best Friends staffers too numerous to name whose paths I crossed along the journey, your dedication was awe-inspiring.

We have a bond, those of us who helped, whether it was behind the scenes, at base camp, on the ground, or from the command center. It is a bond held together by our innate love of animals, no matter how big or small, no matter the breed or species. You are my heroes, one and all. May we never forget the pets of Katrina and strive to ensure that they're never again left behind.

Index

About the Author

Cathy Scott, a veteran journalist, traveled to New Orleans to report the stories of pets displaced by Hurricane Katrina. Best Friends Animal Society, whose work she covered, later hired her as a writer for its magazine and Web sites. She has published one biography and four true-crime books. Her work has appeared in the *New York Times,* the *Los Angeles Times,* the *New York Post,* the  *San Diego Union-Tribune,* the *Las Vegas Sun, George* magazine, and Reuters News Service. Scott, a member of the Society of Professional Journalists' national Speakers Bureau, has appeared on CNN, Court TV, MSNBC, *Unsolved Mysteries,* National Public Radio, and the BBC. She lives in Las Vegas and has a second home in San Diego.